The Witches' Almanac

Spring 2017—Spring 2018

CONTAINING pictorial and explicit delineations of the
magical phases of the Moon together with information about astrological
portents of the year to come and various aspects of occult knowledge
enabling all who read to improve their lives in the old manner.

The Witches' Almanac, Ltd.

Publishers   Providence, Rhode Island
www.TheWitchesAlmanac.com

Address all inquiries and information to
THE WITCHES' ALMANAC, LTD.
P.O. Box 1292
Newport, RI   02840-9998

10-ISBN: 1-881098-39-7

13-ISBN: 978-1-881098-39-3

ISSN: 1522-3184

First Printing July 2016

Printed in USA

Established 1971 by Elizabeth Pepper

8933

Preface

ALTHOUGH MANY WITCHES still choose to work solitary, there are groups that select a common goal and work together. This seems to be the theme over the Internet. Whether in a chat group, through Facebook or just by email, many magicians and witches are pooling their power and working at a predetermined date and time to accomplish what would be harder to do by themselves.

We all know the story of the "Grand Cone of Power" used by Gerald Gardner and others to turn back the forces of Nazi Germany. Some might even recall the astral forces of the Society of Inner Light's founder Dion Fortune. In *The Magical Battle of Britain*, she recounts the story of a time when energy was raised by her, her students and countless witches and magicians all over Britain to achieve one common goal— to defend the island from attack.

We may not be at war on our homeland, but we share this world and the astral with offensive forces, so defense is always a necessary technique to keep readily at hand.

However, power need not be used only for war-defense. At any point in time, power and magic in all of its forms ebbs and flows all around us. We need only gather this power and direct it with our will. When working with a group of practitioners, this is even easier—and more power can be harnessed while the direction the power must take can be made clear.

Consider—when there is a great desire, when a great cause necessitates great action, there needs to be a great power.

HOLIDAYS

Spring 2017 to Spring 2018

Art Director . . . . Gwion Vran

Astrologer . . . . Dikki-Jo Mullen

Climatologist . . . . Tom C. Lang

Cover Art and Design . . . . Kathryn Sky-Peck

Sales . . . . Ellen Lynch

Shipping, Bookkeeping . . . . . D. Lamoureux

ANDREW THEITIC
Executive Editor

GREG ESPOSITO
Managing Editor

JEAN MARIE WALSH
Associate Editor

ANTHONY TETH
Copy Editor

CONTENTS

CONTENTS

A Hymn in Praise of Neptune

Of Neptune's empire let us sing,
At whose command the waves obey;
To whom the rivers tribute pay,
Down the high mountains sliding:
To whom the scaly nation yields
Homage for the crystal fields
Wherein they dwell:
And every sea-god pays a gem
Yearly out of his wat'ry cell
To deck great Neptune's diadem.

The Tritons dancing in a ring
Before his palace gates do make
The water with their echoes quake,
Like the great thunder sounding:
The sea-nymphs chant their accents shrill,
And the sirens, taught to kill
With their sweet voice,
Make ev'ry echoing rock reply
Unto their gentle murmuring noise
The praise of Neptune's empery.

THOMAS CAMPION

7

Yesterday, Today and Tomorrow

by Timi Chasen

IRON OF THE SKY. The treasure trove of King Tutankhamun was filled with dozens of stunningly gorgeous and priceless artifacts. Many were hand crafted by the greatest smiths and jewelers a pharaoh could find, but it appears at least one of ol' Tut's implements may have first fallen from the heavens.

An already priceless dagger found in the collection, resting upon the boy-king's thigh and obviously forged by a master bladesmith, appears to have begun as a venerable piece of meteorite. The blade itself is a combination of iron, nickel and cobalt only found in those pieces of metal which have literally fallen from the sky.

Iron meteorites, though certainly rare, were not unknown to the ancient Egyptians. Around the same time the fireball fell from the stratosphere, a composite hieroglyph began occurring in papyri and inscriptions from the region: "Iron of the Sky." Conveniently the ancients kept detailed historical records, so much so that a combined team of modern Egyptian and Italian researchers had at least twenty documented cases of meteorites making landfall in the land of Khem from which to choose. Eventually, advanced technology was able to confirm its composition to match that of the Kharga meteorite, which landed on a plateau near a seaport approximately 150 miles west of Alexandria.

IS THAT A COIN IN YOUR POCKET? In the remote village of Holmavik rests the Museum of Icelandic Sorcery and Witchcraft. Dedicated to preserving some of the weirder aspects of Icelandic history, the museum exhibits various examples of sorcerous rune carvings, mesmerizing sigil parchments and mysterious spell rel-

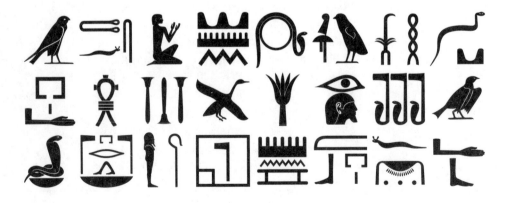

ics from the region, many of them centuries old. Never seen a runic storm charm made from an imposing fish skull? That will be remedied if one stops on by.

The museum's most talked-about attraction is an odd set of pants. Called Necropants, these gruesome slacks were made from human skin and are said to impart wealth and power to their wearer. In life, a person would have made a pact with a sorcerer, bequeathing their lower hide upon death for certain favors. Then, in a complex post-mortem ceremony, the wizard would have carved and peeled the pants from their corpse while using as few cuts as possible. After donning the pants, the sorcerer would insert a special coin in the *ahem* front pouch of the trousers in order to ensure riches came their way. In addition to the pair of grisly undergarments, the museum also hosts a curious stone bowl used to worship the Old Norse Gods, with DNA evidence confirming its use in ritual animal sacrifice—interestingly, the only Norse ritual artifact of its kind so far found with concrete proof of such practices.

NEW HOME FOR OLD GODS. Still north but about 1300 miles east, animal sacrifices to the Norse Gods is precisely how the newly-built Valheim Hof of Denmark opened its doors in May 2016. A temple to Odin and all of the deities of the Old Norse Pantheon, this beautiful wooden structure rises in three tiers surrounded by trees, with a carved dragon head adorning each roof peak.

The opening ceremony involved a sacrifice of nine roosters to the All-Father which were consumed as part of a sacred meal, as well as songs, prayers and supplications to the Gods. Both the Speaker of the Danish Parliament and its Minister of Integration were in attendance, causing a bit of controversy among the more staunchly conservative members of the local government.

The Hof opens up into a beautiful rustic wooden hall with exposed beams and carved wooden accents. A glorious tribute and working temple dedicated to the Deities of old.

UPON THIS ROCK I CARVE MY CHURCH. Though many temples have been built, re-built and renovated over the centuries, very few if any have been carved from a single block of stone. Just such a temple was constructed over 1200 years ago at the behest of Krishna I of the Rashtrakuta Dynasty. Known as the Kailash Temple, this massive feat of

artistic engineering was carved from the top down using only basic hand tools and chisels, with humans and elephants slowly removing over 400,000 tons of stone within the course of two decades. The magnificent multi-tiered result is as impressive as it is stunningly beautiful.

Dedicated to Lord Shiva, the fane includes dozens of inspired representations and illustrated sagas of the deity and attendant animal allies such as sacred bulls and elephants, as well as friezes and statues of other personalities within the pantheon. All of it was executed in exquisite detail with extreme care by brilliant artisans and craftspeople. As if that weren't enough reason to visit, Kailash is merely a single portion of a much larger temple complex known as the Ellora Caves, where 34 other ancient monasteries and temples reside.

CAVE OF WONDER Neanderthals have been getting a bad rap for decades now, stereotyped by most folks to be little more than knuckle-dragging brutes. However, new evidence found at the base of the French Pyrenees may prove them to have had a spiritual side as well.

An ancient rockslide had obscured the entrance to a narrow cave which may contain evidence of religious worship dating deep into the Pleistocene Era. The cave, hidden over 1,100 feet deep underground, consisted of hundreds of stalactite pieces (they kept most of the stalagmites intact), carefully broken and arranged in a series of rings. Throughout the cave there was also evidence of numerous fires and the bones of bears and other animals arranged in neat piles, in a manner hinting at religious reverence.

The astonishing age of the structure's limestone formations came about through a special technique of uranium dating, able to pinpoint the time the stalactites were broken off of the ceiling, since carbon dating processes apparently lack accuracy for determining the age of anything older than 50,000 years. How old did the stalactites turn out to be through this process—175,000 years or so, give or take a millennium or two, making it well more than 100,000 years older than the earliest cave paintings we've ever found. The only hominids anywhere near the area at that time were, you guessed it, Neanderthals.

GREEN DRAGON KINGDOM. Bhutan, a landlocked country residing on the Eastern end of the Himalayan range, is known for its graceful Buddhist temples and breathtaking mountain landscapes. Now, it is coming to be known as the only carbon negative developing country in the world. This is due to both to its strict environmental laws as well as scores of its

caring citizens. Apparently, approximately 72 percent of the entire country is forested, with measures built into the constitution ensuring that at least 60 percent will remain wild and unmolested.

In addition, the country's inhabitants are more than willing to plant trees en masse. A team of 100 Bhutanese, in honor of the 60th birthday of their 4th Dragon King who abdicated the throne to his son, broke a world record by planting 49,672 trees in one hour. More recently 82,000 households planted trees in honor of the current Dragon Queen's first child.

It is said the kingdom of approximately 750,000 people produces about 1.5 billion tons of carbon dioxide each year, while its extensive mountainous woodlands have the ability to nullify the impact of over four times that amount.

SOL COUGHING. Scientists have been paying close attention to some dark spots on the Sun's surface recently. Called *coronal holes*, these massive discolorations can only be spotted with specialized infrared technology and apparently have the potential to cause some serious damage.

Generally, our nearest star's perpetual nuclear combustion creates a series of magnetic fields which tend to loop up and then back down toward its surface. What has NASA worried is that these coronal holes appear to be instances where those fields are instead shot out into the void. Considering the potency of these expulsions, astronauts fear they may actually damage life-supporting equipment and communications in space, while some scientists worry that if sent out at the right trajectory, these runaway magnetic fields may also seriously damage satellite and communication technology here on Earth.

Unfortunately, only time will tell if Sol's less stable manifestations will cause problems for our friendly explorers of the stars. Until then, "Houston" has their eyes peeled. Let us hope these emanations disrupt little more than a stray Twitter feed or two.

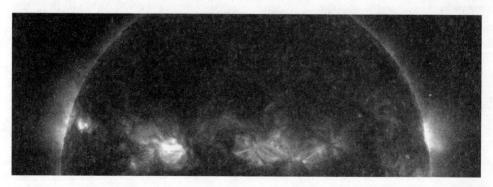

The Blessed Raven

A tale of a talking head and a cauldron

THE STORY of Bendigeidfran (Bran the Blessed or more literally The Blessed Raven) is one of the fantastical happenings of an ancient divinely bred king, a giant of stature and ability, his regenerative magical cauldron and his prophetic disembodied head.

As related by the storytellers of Ancient Prydain, Bran the Blessed wished to forge an alliance with the Island of Erin (Ireland) and so gave his sister Branwen in betrothal to Matholwch the King of Ireland. Now Bran the Blessed in his hubris failed to consult his half-brother Efnisien. On hearing of his exclusion from such an important decision, Efnisien became enraged. As the wedding feast ensued, he stole away from festivities and maimed the horses of the Irish king Matholwch in revenge of the slight. Efnisien's actions were such an offense that Bran the Blessed had no choice but to offer the Irish king his most prized possession, his wondrous magical cauldron, in reparation. Matholwch though vexed accepted the compensation and set off to his homeland with his new wife in tow and an apparent alliance in place.

Matholwch arrived back in Erin

satisfied with the apology, however his court and people would not forget so easily the insults hoisted upon the King and the people of Erin. However, time would bide the issue for a bit. Several years passed and the sister of Bran the Blessed bore to Matholwch and the people of Erin a prince who was given the name Gwern. With an heir procured for the people of Erin, Matholwch was reminded of the insult visited on him at the court of Bran and was soon persuaded to banish Branwen from the court to work as a scullery maid in the kitchens. To further the insult to the high born Branwen, each day she was beaten and her ears boxed by the butcher.

Matholwch decreed that no man should be allowed to travel to Prydain, for fear and as an assurance that news of Branwen's mistreatment would not reach Bran the Blessed's court. Branwen in her desperation trained a starling to carry news to her brother. Bran was indeed angered when the starling relayed the message and immediately gathered his army to cross to Erin. Now such was Bran the

12

Blessed's stature that there was not a boat that could accommodate his great size, so he waded across the sea alongside his retinue.

Matholwch's sentinels saw a great shape making its way towards Erin and warned the king of the approaching danger. The King of Erin immediately knew the Giant of Prydain was coming to avenge his sister, so Matholwch and his court made their way to the west of the great island retreating for fear of their fate at the hands of the giant. The mighty forces of Bran the Blessed pursued the King of Erin's retinue, crossing all the mighty rivers of Erin, even the Linon River. Matholwch set his magicians to work, enchanting the river with a lodestone to drag any passing ship into the depths. Bran the Blessed read the omens and immediately stretched his giant body across the Linon bank to bank so his men could march over him, cornering the Irish king and his court.

At last cornered, Matholwch sued for peace and offered to abdicate in favor of his son and Bran's nephew, Gwern. Bran accepted the terms of peace, additionally insisting that a great public celebration should take place and the people of Erin should build a great house that could not only host a grand feast but accommodate Bran the Blessed's great stature. Matholwch and his advisors quickly agreed and set the feast.

The court of Matholwch convinced him to again complicate the situation. They would place one hundred soldiers in leather sacks and hang them like bags of flour from the pillars of the great hall, thus planning a surprise attack once the feast had begun. These assassins would jump out and murder Bran as he ate. Efnisien immediately saw through the ploy and immediately questioned the contents of the sacks. Feeling the head of a man within one he pinched it, crushing the assassin's skull. He gave all one hundred sacks the same treatment until all the would-be murderers were

dispatched, telling no one of the actual contents. In one final act of retribution, again haste driven by rage, Efnisien thrust Gwern the newly crowned king of Erin into the great fire set in the hearth of the hall, killing the boy.

The battle that ensued was indeed a bloody one and the soldiers of Erin would have been defeated readily, save for the magicians of Matholwch's court. They knew the secret of the magic cauldron gifted to their king by Bran the Blessed. It was the Cauldron of Rebirth, reanimating the lifeless bodies of the fallen soldiers once they were placed into the cauldron. But even the cauldron could not save the men of Erin, for in an act of contrition Efnisien threw himself into the cauldron and pushed with all his might against the sides, bursting the cauldron and sacrificing himself. Only the dead could go into the Cauldron of Rebirth, the living had no place in it. Bran the Blessed's retinue were victorious, killing the entirety of Erin save seven pregnant women who would be the future of the now defeated Kingdom of Erin.

While Bran the Blessed's retinue were victorious, celebration was not to be had. There were only seven surviving from Prydain and the great giant had been wounded with a dolorous blow to the heel by a poisoned spear. Bran the Blessed survived long enough to request his head be cut off and be taken back to his homeland. It was then that the men of Prydain realized Bran was indeed of the otherworld. His disembodied head instructed them to bring his head back to Caer-Lundein (London) where they would bury it in Gwynfryn (The White Mount). There, his head would protect Prydain for eternity, as long as it remained undisturbed.

Though an enormous retinue had travelled to Erin, only eight returned with the head, one of which was Branwen. When Branwen reached Prydain she died of the great grief she carried in her heart. The head of Bran the Blessed gave one further instruction to the brave seven; they were to retire to Harlech. They did so and for seven years the head of Bran continued to provide them with stories and prophecy, the seven men not perceiving the passing of time. This continued until at last one of the men opened the eastward facing door, immediately realizing that their charge must be completed.

The seven made their way to Caer-Lundein and buried the head in the White Mount facing the continent. There it stayed protecting Prydain until Arthur's arrogance would have otherwise.

Thus ends the story of the giant Bran the Blessed.

Story retold by
–GWION VRAN

Collect the Whole Set...
of Gods

REMEMBER the line from toy ads, "Collect the whole set?" Who would have thought it would apply to Gods? But, when we invoke each of the deities and spirits in turn, we enter into an ancient path of profound spiritual advancement, drawing ever closer to the source of being.

This technique can be traced back through time to C.E. 300. In a book we call *On the Mysteries*, a Syrian prince named Iamblichus wrote about this method as a path of spiritual development. The purpose of the book was to defend traditional religious practices, but it also explained some of the advanced forms of spirituality of the day called 'theurgy.'

Iamblichus was strongly influenced by Pythagoras, treating him as a profound authority on matters spiritual, social and physical. Pythagoras seems to be the first to explain the principle of whole systems, showing that totalities often have properties unpredictable from examining their parts. Today this kind of thinking is called 'systems theory.' The pieces working together to produce the unpredicted is called 'synergy,' and the possible results are called 'emergent properties.'

From this principle Iamblichus counseled the spiritual explorer to invoke all of the Gods. Meaning we are to invoke all of the deities and spirits of all the realms—Terrestrial, Celestial and Divine, as well as all the local spirits and the spirits of nations. He goes to significant lengths in *De Mysteriis* to explain the many classes of Gods and spirits, how they relate to each other and how they all fit into the cosmic scheme. Through invoking them all, we build positive relations with all of the world and are better able to live in harmony with it.

But, when the world is full of Gods, as the pre-Socratic philosopher Thales said, there are a lot of Gods to invoke. This is where the 'sets' come in. By invoking one limited group at a time, or rather each part of a set until it is

completed, we leverage this principle of wholeness and gain its benefits without having to track down every spiritual being in the neighborhood.

Invoking Often

This process begins by invoking the elements. Of course, one must first learn how, but assuming they have developed the skill, the trick is to intensely invoke the four classical elements: air, fire, water and earth, one at a time. Intensely cannot be overemphasized: three times per day for thirty days running (or a Moon cycle) is about the minimum to get the proper effect. No banishing, if you can help it. You want to build the presence of the element and imbalance yourself as much as possible without doing damage. After having invoked just one for a month, move on to the next.

It is best to start out with a month's worth of invocation of all four elements together as a way of tuning up the practice. Then, each element is given a month alone. After all four have been individually invoked, one returns to invoking all four in the same ritual.

Something amazing emerges. First and more obviously, one discovers a balance that can only come after progressive and deep imbalance. More importantly, the Quintessence arises. There is no way to explain this, but it is the source and sum of the other four elements. In the synergy of the four, the fifth shines forth as an emergent property. A new awareness of the life that pervades the physical, terrestrial world, dawns in the invoker's soul. From this entry into the Terrestrial also comes the first steps toward the Solar core and the opening of the Celestial.

Only by establishing deep relation with the Terrestrial, can access to the Celestial be obtained. But with it, as though you can finally stand on it rather than be submerged in it, the Terrestrial points directly to the Sun, the core of the Celestial system. Now it is time to invoke the planets. This is done differently: we live in a culture in which each day of the week is named for a planet and by working with the classical seven we tie into one of the fundamental levels of our culture, if one forgotten by most folk these days. Invoke one planet per day for at least six months, ideally a year. Because of the rulerships of the zodiacal signs by the planets, the starry part of the Celestial system is included; you might wish to name them while doing your planetary invocations.

When you have completed establishing your relationships with the Celestial Ones, the Empyrean opens before you. This is the realm of the Gods themselves. Depending on your pantheon, your approach may vary, but if you like the Qabalah, invoking the deities of the Ten Sephiroth will accomplish this stage. How long you do this is between you and the Gods. By this point you will have enough skill to listen to their instruction. Follow it.

Expanding Mind and Soul

Besides the obvious educational value of such a cycle of practice, Iamblichus taught that by activating the presence of all the Gods within your soul, which this does, it makes you into a microcosm of the macrocosm that is the Universe. With it a deep resonance arises between you and the whole of being. You begin to feel and not just know your place in the world.

You experience the plural presence of the divine in all things, times and places. Likewise, as you advance you come to understand your part in the administration of the cosmos of which you are an integral part.

On a more psychological level, by invoking all of these divinities, you come to know yourself better and balance out the parts of your personality, each part getting their due. Lacks in your personality become filled, excesses tempered. You become more whole.

What Iamblichus and the ancients of his day taught was that it is well and good to invoke the Gods at their respective feasts and holy days, but to advance spiritually, we need to know all Gods and make them a part of our lives and ourselves. This working with the Gods they called 'theurgy' or 'god-work,' and it gives new meaning to the line, 'Collect the Whole Set.'

–SAM WEBSTER

Hocus Pocus

or The Anatomy of Legerdemain
and A Dark Composure Of Words

"WHAT DOES Hocus Pocus mean?"

The question came as a surprise. It was the first one asked by one of the movie-goers at the Wednesday night film club, hosted by The Winter Park Library near Orlando, Florida. This popular weekly event provides free movies to the community followed by a discussion led by guest speakers knowledgeable about the plot of the film featured that night. It was just before Halloween and following the delightful 1993 Disney film *Hocus Pocus*. The movie stars Bette Midler as a snaggle-toothed crone leading a trio of time traveling witch sisters through a Halloween adventure in Salem, Massachusetts.

Today the phrase Hocus Pocus has become synonymous with foolish diversions. Hocus Pocus makes us think of something designed to distract and deceive, turning attention away from what is really happening. It has been used by a Canadian newspaper to describe the actions of politicians with unpopular hidden agendas. On the surface this definition of the film's title does vaguely fit. The story line is a comedy which includes a series of amusing mishaps.

However the phrase has been in use since at least 1622 and contains an array of deeper hints and subtleties. Hocus Pocus might be derived from an ancient and lost language. It has been spoken aloud by conjurers and magicians as they performed supernatural feats and changes for at least four hundred years. Several early 17th century plays used the term, most notably *The Masque of Augeres* by Ben Johnson. The first book published in English about illusion dates from 1634, its title was *Hocus Pocus Junior, The Anatomy of Legerdemain* by William Vincent. It is interesting to note that legerdemain is an early English word for magic. The author was a famous conjurer of the era. He was first granted a license to perform magic in 1619 and eventually was appointed to the Court as personal magician to King James. Vincent's book was so popular that it went through numerous editions.

In 1655 Thomas Addy wrote in his book *A Candle in the Dark or, a*

Treatise Concerning the Nature of Witches and Witchcraft:

> *"I will speak of one man* (William Vincent) *that went about in King James his time who called himself, The Kings Majesties most excellent Hocus Pocus, and was so called, because at the playing of every trick, he used to say "Hocus Pocus, tontus talontus, vade celeriter jubeo, a dark composure of words to blinde the eyes of the beholders, to make his Trick pass the more currently without discovery."*

At that time magic was not separated from performances by jugglers, jesters and other performers.

By 1694 John Tillotson, Archbishop of Canterbury, suggested the magical words Hocus Pocus were actually from a corrupt form of the consecration of the communion host in the early Latin Mass, *hoc est corpus meum*, translated as "this is my body." Even during the 17th century this idea was considered far-fetched and met with considerable skepticism. Archbishop Tillotson was an Anglican, so he might have been attacking Catholics as well as Witches and magicians in his sermons.

Over the years the phrase Hocus Pocus became the trademark for superior magic. It might simply have begun as an invention, inspired by William Vincent, to add an impressive aura of mystery and drama to his performances. However according to Sharon Turner, author of *The History of the Anglo Saxons* (four volumes, 1799–1805), Hocus Pocus was derived from the name Ochus Bochus, a magician and demon from the North. In Russia a derivation of Hocus Pocus becomes *fokus*, a word for trickery. In Scandinavia, Holland and Russia a variant spelling, *filipokus*, is common.

Although the origins and exact meaning of the mysterious phrase Hocus Pocus remain forever unclear, it has frequently been chanted by magicians over the centuries to facilitate a change or breakthrough. A bit of Hocus Pocus certainly brought success to magical efforts in earlier times. Contemporary witches who are drawn to the mystique and possible latent power of magical words and phrases might want to experiment by chanting "Hocus Pocus" or even the complete phrase, "Hocus Pocus, tontus talontus, vade celeriter jubeo."

—Esther Elayne

19

Faith and Belief in Traditional British Old Craft

NATURAL OLD CRAFT abilities are not governed by any form of religious allegiance but rather by the channeling of natural energies or powers of Nature. Those who acted in a priestly or shamanic capacity for our Pretannic ancestors probably saw these natural forces as more abstract concepts than we do today. For them, masculine energy would be seen in terms of the hunter-protector-rutter, while feminine energy would manifest in more general terms of fecundity and the hearth. And because mankind has always had a tendency to see images of its gods in his own likeness, we have come to see pagan deities very much cast in 20th century form.

What it is important to understand, however, is that neither Wicca nor the modern trend of eclectic paganism is synonymous with Old Craft. It may utilize many of the *trappings* but Old Craft will *always* be a matter of ability, not religious conviction. In purely magical terms, it is not possible to upend these ancient concepts just because they are at odds with 20th century political correctness. A traditional British Old Craft witch was probably, more often than not, seen taking part in Christian observances, and still refers to the seasonal festivals by the 'mass' celebrated within the church calendar of the time.

The 'God of the Witches' concept was one coined by Margaret Murray in her book of the same name, first published in 1931 as an anthropological study. Around the same time, Gerald Gardner inaugurated the tradition that we now know as 'Gardnerian,' based on alleged rituals from a group practicing in the

New Forest. Margaret Murray endorsed these claims by penning the Preface to Gardner's own book, *Witchcraft Today*, a rag-bag of folklore, superstition, history and anthropology but the elevation of the 'goddess' within Gardnerian rituals was predominantly his own.

For the purposes of Old Craft technique it is important to accept the energies associated with the male-female aspects of magic and not transpose the concept of the loving, caring mother-goddess of Wicca-Christianity into Old Craft working. The female-goddess energy within Nature is just as red in tooth and claw as male-god energy; each is equally as merciless as the other. It is also important to understand that this energy (whether male or female) is neither malevolent nor benevolent, it is merely *natural energy* waiting to be harnessed for use in Old Craft magic.

Horned God, Veiled Goddess

Old Craft, although not a religion, is a belief—a belief in one's own abilities and in the 'Power' that fuels the Universe; and a faith—faith in one's own abilities and that same 'Power.' This is not generally seen as gender specific but in truth, Old Craft does lean towards the male aspect since the female remains veiled and a mystery. In other words, the 'God' is the public face of traditional British Old Craft while the 'Goddess' remains in the shadows, revered and shielded by her protector. Not because she is some shy and defenseless creature but because face to face she would be too terrible to look upon! Or as the scientist who discovered the deadly Marburg filovirus observed when he saw the viral particles (*The Hot Zone*, Richard Preston): "They were white cobras tangled among themselves, like the hair of Medusa. They were the face of Nature herself, the obscene goddess revealed naked… breathtakingly beautiful." The secrets of Old Craft comes from the understanding of these things because it is not possible to convey the true meanings of our Ways to a *cowan* or 'outsider' who has not experienced these Mysteries for themselves.

Our witchcraft has taught us a basic tenet of belief that although not a religion, there is a highly defined spiritual element to its practice. Also that traditional British Old Craft—like the mysteries of pre-dynastic Egypt and pre-Roman Italy, the ancestral beliefs of Japanese Shinto, the Aboriginal tribes of Australia and the indigenous Native Americans— is fundamentally animistic. Animism is, of course, the belief that every object, animate and inanimate, has its own life-force or energy. Here there is no separation between the spiritual or physical world, where 'spirit' exists in all flora and fauna (including humans); geological features such as rocks, mountains, rivers and springs; and in natural phenomena such as storms, wind and the movement of heavenly bodies. It is the understanding that a small quartz pebble can link us with the cosmic Divine.

Shamanic Roots

Taking this viewpoint into account, it is not unreasonable to claim that Old Craft is probably the native shamanic practice of the British Isles. The term 'shamanism' describing the supernatural powers practitioners channel from the spirit world for healing, divination and the conducting of souls—all of which are the natural province of an Old Craft witch where it is viewed as 'an isolated or peripheral phenomenon,' rather than the overt devotional practices often found in contemporary Wicca. As intermediaries between the world of the Ancestors and the living, the Old Craft witch maintains direct contact with spirits, whether of Otherworld, plants, animals and other features of the environment, such as the 'master-spirits' (e.g. of rivers or mountains).

A natural witch also has the ability to identify and interact with this spirit energy on which the Witch must draw for all purposes of Craft practice. Without this natural ability there is no Old Craft witch, because as Hotspur retorts to Glendower's claim he can 'call spirits from the vasty deep.' "Why, so can I, or so can any man; but will they come when you do call for them?" And, which particular spirit energy do we conjure for what purpose? The gentle ethereal energy of the fields and hedgerows differs quite considerably from the primitive and often menacing energy of the woods and forests or the ever-changing seashore, while mountains and rivers generate their own mystique.

The most powerful energy on which an Old Craft witch can call, however, is that of our 'Ancestors' who represent our culture, traditions, heritage, lineage and antecedents; they trace the long march of history that our predecessors have taken under the aegis of traditional British Old Craft. When those of a particular Tradition pass beyond the veil, their spiritual essence merges with the divine spirit of the Whole, which in turn gives traditional Witchcraft the continuing power to endure—even past its own time and place in history. It therefore remains the duty of an Old Craft witch to ensure the soul of any newly deceased can successfully join the Ancestors and keep adding to the strength of belief which, in many instances, may already have endured for hundreds of years.

If we cannot acknowledge and respect the Ancestors of traditional British Old Craft to which we *claim* to belong when living, then we will contribute nothing to the Whole when we die. Reverence for Craft Ancestors is part of the ethic of respect for those who have preceded us in life, and their continued presence on the periphery

of our consciousness means they are always with us. And because traditional witchcraft is essentially a practical thing, the Ancestors are called upon to help find solutions to magical problems through divination, path-working and spell-casting.

Nevertheless, Bob Clay-Egerton brought everything full circle (*Coven of the Scales: The Collected Writings of A R Clay-Egerton*) when he described the Power of the One in pure animistic terms. "The Almighty is everything, physical and non-physical, literally everything and therefore incomprehensible to our finite understanding. Being everything, the Almighty is male and female and neuter—not just a male entity. All things are created in the image of the Almighty because the Almighty is every part of everything. The Almighty has no specific regard or concern for one species—for example mankind, among millions of species on one insignificant minor planet, in an outer arm of a spiral galaxy which is one among millions."

Traditional British Old Craft remains an oral tradition and much can still be found in our native folklore that resonates with those schooled in this more primitive form of witchcraft not reliant on group dynamics and psycho-drama to raise magical energy. And while an Old Craft witch can continue to find solace amongst the forests and woodland, lakes and mountains, in the rural landscape and on the seashore, the spirit-energies that power our belief will continue to endure.

–MELUSINE DRACO

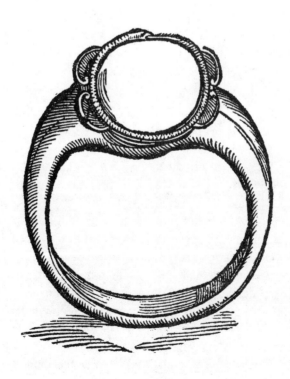

The Sacred Acre

The Magic of the Land Between Low and High Tide

"Tell him to buy me an acre of land,
  Parsley, sage, rosemary, and thyme;
  Between the salt water and the sea sand,
  Then he shall be a true lover of mine."
  —*Scarborough Fair (Simon & Garfunkel variant, 1966)*

"Ye'll get an acre o gude red-land
  Atween the saut sea and the sand."
  —*The Elfin Knight (variant 2C around 1650, perhaps older)*

"One day the lad fared forth till he was on the brink of the sea - for the poets
deemed that on the brink of water it was always a place of revelation of science."
  —*The Colloquy of the Two Sages (Druid teaching tale from around 800)*

THERE IS A PLACE called the Sacred Acre which is the land that lies between the marks of the low tide and the marks of the high tide. It is the land that belongs to both the spirits of the Sea and the spirits of the Land. The Sacred Acre, like the tides, is always in flux as it moves along the seashores of the world. As it shifts, its shape and size changes. As it moves, it travels through the hours of day and night, through all the phases of the Moon and seasons of the Sun. The Sacred Acre is the moving threshold, the walking crossroads, the liminal place where many realms and reali-ties meet. As such it has been and will always be a place where magick can be wrought. This is a very powerful place. What would normally take many rituals, invocations, complicated preparations or convoluted sigils can often be done in an hour with no more than a driftwood wand. If you live near the sea, then you will have a task to perform. If you live far from the sea, a pilgrimage to make. If you cannot make it to the sea then the way is harder, but there is still a way.

If you have the good fortune to live near the sea, then begin by finding places on the shore that are quieter, less

crowded and private. Take time to explore the area you select and let the sense of the place seep into you through your senses. Pick up the local newspaper or go online and make it a habit to keep track of the local tides. When you are standing on the land between the boundaries of the tides, breathe in the salt air and feel how energy moves through you. Become aware of how the energy feels when the tide is coming in, when it is going out and in the quiet and churn that is the transition between tides. Open your subtle senses and become aware of the spirits of the sea and land that gather on the Sacred Acre. Come prepared to leave them offerings such as a pinch of soil from near your home, flowers, rainwater you collected or any other natural gift that means something to you. When you trust you are in alignment with the powers gathering on the seashore, then proceed with whatever ritual, working or divination you desire. Always offer thanks and a farewell to all the seen and unseen that have witnessed and assisted your work before departing.

If you live far from the sea and your time at the shore will be brief, then it must be treated as an important pilgrimage. Before departing for the journey, take a purification bath. Choose clothing and jewelry that has a symbolic meaning for you. You need not wear robes or overtly occult jewelry, strangers around you do not need to know what you are doing. Though do not be surprised if other witches and pagans take notice of the symbolism of what you are wearing as a pilgrim to the sea.

When you get to the shore, as soon as your feet are upon the sand, pause and silently or aloud introduce yourself to the Sacred Acre and all the beings that dwell there. If you had more time, you could slowly build up a relationship with the place, but since time is short a formal introduction is quickest. Then, with whatever time you have for your pilgrimage, follow the same steps that were given for those that live close to the shore. Before departing, give one more offering and you may scoop up a small quantity of sand and salt water into a jar. Do not forget to offer thanks. When you return home place the jar upon an altar decorated with emblems of the sea. Study the tides of the place from which you took a piece of the Sacred Acre. Touch the sand and salt water at different tides and know you are touching the seashore however many miles away it may be. In time, your altar to the Sacred Acre will become imbued with power. Do not be surprised if you hear the cry of a gull within your home.

If life circumstances prevent you from going to the ocean, there are still ways to connect to the power of the sea and to tread upon the Sacred Acre. Through purchases or gifts brought by friends, collect and assemble an altar to the sea. Next acquire sea salt from a specific place. Sea salt with no specific provenance will not do. There are many gourmet shops that sell sea salt from particular locations. Pick a spot on the sea that provided the salt and look up its tides. If you can find photos of the seashore from the spot you picked, place them on your sea altar. Now the magic can begin.

All life on the land arose from the sea. You were formed in the salty water of your mother's womb whose cycles were called by the Moon. The salt in your blood remembers the sea. The sea is always with you. You just need to remember this and know it is true. When you believe it, put a grain or two of the sea salt on your tongue. Look at the tide charts and envision the Sacred Acre. Feel the sea breeze and hear the crash of the waves. Let the rhythmic pulse of the sea's power move within you. With practice, with time and tide, you'll be able to stand on the Sacred Acre within yourself.

The Sacred Acre is a place that is always changing yet very specific. It is found throughout the world, but is also between the worlds. The Sacred Acre is born of the dance of Sun, Moon and Earth and is motion made manifest. It is the place where sea, sky and land greet the fire of your spirit in the stillness and the roaring of eternal continuance. The Sacred Acre is like a cast circle, a great temple, a bubble of sea foam in the great sea of infinity. What can you do in the

Sacred Acre? The scope of what you can do in the Sacred Acre is the same as how much you can become it, a grain of sand or the whole of the ocean.

Whatever your path or tradition may be, it would be wise to visit the Sacred Acre. Whether it be to refresh your spirit and reconnect with the powers of nature, or whether it be the start of one of your regular ways of power, many a witch has come into their own on the seashore. Do not rush this work and do remember your offerings and gratitude. You will be rewarded by gifts that can only be given by this sacred portal.

—Ivo Dominguez Jr.

BINDING SPELLS

Eight words the Wiccan Rede fulfill

An it harm none, do what thou will

The Wiccan Rede

SIMILAR to a doctor's oath, the Wiccan Rede admonishes its adherents to harm none. But what if someone is harming others and needs to be stopped? Is one justified to perform a death spell to protect the community?

From the number of curses documented throughout history, it's clear that at one time, witches didn't hesitate to lay a death curse if they felt justified. Cattle thieves and even romantic rivals could find themselves at the end of a magickal blast.

To stop a person from performing a certain action without necessarily harming him or her, witches with more compassion used what are commonly called binding spells. There are also spells that bind people together, as in a handfasting, but here we will discuss only the type of binding spells that stop actions.

Constrictive Constructs

The ancient Romans and Greeks wrote binding spells on tablets of wax or lead, describing the action to be prevented. A curse tablet found in Athens bound the "tongue... soul... and ...speech" of three people who were to testify in a trial so they would not speak out against the defendant.

Later, the Greeks and Romans graduated to crude figurines formed of wax, clay, or sewn from pieces of cloth. This is what we find today. The witch using an effigy to represent the person doing the harm and performing the binding spell on it, usually during a waning moon.

Traditionally, a sample of the person's handwriting, a piece of hair, fingernail clippings or even the dirt from the person's footprint would be added to the doll to strengthen the link between the intended and its representation. After the advent of photography, a photograph would be added.

Some witches consider a photograph or handwriting sample sufficient. Some consider the hand-formed effigy to be more potent because of the energy and concentration needed to form it, the important thing being intent. If the witch can concentrate and form intent while staring at a photograph or writing sample, then they will do.

The Rite Approach

To begin the spell, the witch calls the item by the person's name and states aloud that whatever is done to the item is done to the person the item represents. The witch then performs an act of sympathetic magick.

For example, to silence someone

who is spreading lies or making a work environment intolerable by constantly bickering, a witch might sew or tape the mouth shut. To stop someone who keeps swiping their lunch out of the company kitchen, a witch might tie or tape the hands together. To prevent a person or animal from straying, a witch might bind the legs. To stop a rapist, a witch might tape the genitals.

Example of a Binding Spell

In the case of someone taking advantage of an elderly person, the witch might sew or tape the mouth shut (to prevent the person from verbally conning the victim), bind the hands with thread or tape (to prevent the person from stealing or forging signatures on checks), or even bind the feet to prevent the person from going to the elder's house.

As the witch completes each action, she tells the poppet what she is doing. "With this tape, I seal shut your mouth, John Smith, so that you may no longer convince Ruth to give you money or valuables. With this tape, I bind your hands that you may no longer forge her signature on her social security check. With this tape, I bind your feet so that you may no longer visit her and trouble her."

As with all magick, the witch must take care. In our example, if the witch binds the abuser too early, the police may not see any evidence of a crime and the person may leave, only to abuse someone else. Or, if the suspected abuser is not the real abuser, by binding his mouth, hands and feet, the witch might prevent him from discovering or stopping the real abuser.

Ethics of Binding

Some modern witches avoid any spells that interfere with a person's will, even if it would stop an undesired action. They believe interfering with the free will of another is interfering with that person's destiny or karma.

Yet others believe that if someone is causing harm and non-magickal efforts (like calling the police) are delayed or ineffective, a binding is justified. Some go even further and condone a binding any time harm must be stopped, carefully crafting the wording of the binding spell so the wrong person won't be arrested for a crime.

Consequences of Binding

Even when a witch takes care with the technical aspects of a spell, things may go awry. The spell may be done too late, after the damage is done. The witch might bind the wrong person or the wording of the spell may have unnoticed loopholes. An example might be a witch being too specific and binding a person from forging a signature on a social security check, but not on other types of checks.

Conversely, the wording might not be specific enough, binding the person against speaking, without specifying harmful speech.

When witches perform a spell, they accept whatever consequences occur and therefore should not use binding spells lightly.

–Nevrom Ydal

Greaco-Egyptian Magic

ONE MIGHT THINK modern witchcraft has very little to do with the magic practiced by Graeco-Egyptian magicians during Roman times in ancient Egypt (the first five centuries C.E.), but one would be mistaken. Surprisingly, magical techniques have changed very little over the centuries. Driving a nail through an inscribed lead plate before nailing it to the wall or casting it into a river is as likely to be part of a modern witch's repertoire as it was part of the workings of magicians living in the city of Alexandria, Egypt 1800 years ago. This particular technique, called a *defixio*, was practiced throughout the Roman Empire from France to Egypt, but its source was the unique blend of Greek and Egyptian magic to be found in the *Graeco-Egyptian Magical Papyri* (*PGM* for short).

A *defixio* was used to bind enemies or slow down athletes (typically charioteers) belonging to an opposing team, or more frequently to attract or bind a lover. They were also used to bind the tongues of witnesses who might speak against the magician in court, all objectives as viable today as they were thousands of years ago.

What is so special about the Graeco-Egyptian papyri? The papyri contain more on what is to be said and done, better explaining the mechanism

that makes the spell work in detail, than most modern sources of magical lore. In the case of the *defixio* it relies upon a daemon or the spirit of someone newly or untimely dead. It is for this reason that a *defixio*, once nailed, was supposed to be secreted in a river, or better still a tomb (as entrance to the Underworld), rather than simply nailed up on a barn door. It is only in the papyri of the Graeco-Egyptian magicians that the method and mechanism are spelled out in full. What has come down to us is simply inscribing a metal plate with a spell and then using a nail to fix it. What is missing is the rationale behind this act, the correct placement of the plate and the exact words to be said. These details are however still extant in the papyri.

Magic Scrolls

The bulk of these papyri were discovered in a tomb in Thebes, and they were almost certainly the library of a practicing magician of that era. They contain 581 different "spells" in 13,639 lines of carefully written Greek. "Spells" has been placed in quotes because this is often the word used by translators for a variety of operations, since the English language is not well endowed with words for different types of magic. In the original Greek there are more than 40 different words attached to as many precisely different magical methods, all varying in method, but all simply translated as "spell." For example, there are more than seven types of love spell, each with its own name. An *agōgē* is a magical practice designed to lead the loved one to the magician, figuratively referred to as "love's leash"; but an *agōgimon* is designed to compel the loved one to come immediately to the magician's home; and an *agrupnētikon* threatens to keep the loved one from either sleep or food until they give in. It is perhaps not important to know these names, just to understand that the spells given in the *PGM* contain so much more detail than their descendants which have survived 1800 years of church inspired persecution and destruction.

Enduring Methods

It is extraordinary that while mankind usually discards methods that don't work, many of these methods of magic used by the ancient Egyptian magicians are alive, well and being practised today. Some of the most interesting methods outlined are those for skrying. The Graeco-Egyptian magicians used both the flame of a lamp and the surface of a liquid in a copper bowl upon which oil had been floated. But they did not for a moment think it was sufficient to simply stare into the flame or bowl and let the mind go blank. Instead they actively conjured a daemon or spirit (or even a god) to give them true answers to the questions they posed. Furthermore, they outlined techniques for both solitary work and for using a virgin child as a skryer.

The invocations for this purpose are given and even a method for rapidly throwing the child into trance.

These methods endured in the Greek world for another thousand years where they became part of the classical Greek grimoire the *Hygromanteia*. Dr John Dee and his skryer Edward Kelley used some of these methods but chose to call them angels rather than daemons and replaced the copper bowl of water and oil with a crystal. The ancients (especially the Chinese) thought of crystal as the 'water-stone.' The *Hygromanteia* in turn became famous as the ancestor of *The Key of Solomon*, which was first published in English by MacGregor Mathers, one of the founders of the Golden Dawn. Meanwhile the skrying methods became detached from the grimoires and turn up in Trithemius' book *On the Art of Drawing Spirits into Crystals*. This book has in turn inspired the work of one of the foremost experimental magicians of this day, Frater Ashen Chassan.

Treading Carefully

In the *PGM*, the later medieval grimoires and the *Key of Solomon*, there is a strong emphasis on protection against the spirits. It is not a good idea to call them up casually, without any protection, as the result of this can be obsession or at the least mental imbalance. The ancient Graeco-Egyptian magicians often worked inside a consecrated temple and wore a *phylakterion* on their chests. The ancient Jewish high priest also wore a breastplate for spiritual protection and almost all the mediaeval grimoires recommend a *lamen* to be worn in the same way.

When not inside a consecrated temple, the Graeco-Egyptian magicians used a circle on the floor in the form of an ouroboros, or serpent swallowing its tail. The magic circle is an essential part of grimoire evocation ritual, and one late manuscript of the *Goetia* even shows the circle in the form of a serpent with words of power inscribed upon its length, but sadly not swallowing its tail. Even today Witches traditionally

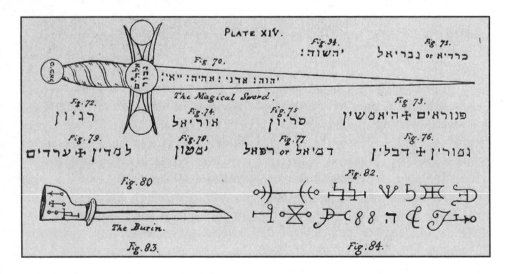

cast a circle before beginning to work.

These spells are all translated into English in Hans Betz's *The Greek Magical Papyri in Translation*, an extremely useful volume. But, it has one big drawback, the spells are all mixed up, just in the order they happened to be written, with invocations mixed up with suggestions for removing a fish bone stuck in the throat, or something to provoke dreams, skry or cure a dog bite. The solution is to use the Greek subheadings that were applied by the original author to unscramble them, but these are often just translated as 'spell.' To solve that problem, comb through each of the extant papyri and extract the more than 40 different Greek terms for the different techniques that were in regular use by Graeco-Egyptian magicians. Then, using these subheadings, one could sort all the 'spells' into their different categories.

–Dr. Stephen Skinner

A Bee Keeper's Year

January—Bees are somnolent unless it's warm (45–50 degrees), so this is the time to make new frames and fill supers. Each hive needs about twenty five pounds of stored honey this month. When it snows, check to keep the hive entrance open. Read up on bee keeping and consider which flowers and trees to plant. Attend a bee club meeting. Order new bees. Ask the highway department to plant wild flowers along roads and median strips instead of mowing.

February—The queen begins laying and the hive is comprised of only females. The bees need another twenty five pounds of stored honey. Go to bee club meetings and discuss preserving fields of wildflowers in your community instead of mowing. Petition local businesses to landscape with wild flowers rather than grass. Ask the electric company to stop spraying under power lines.

March—Examine colonies and remove dead bees. Start feeding with pollen, honey, granulated sugar if the weather is cold, cane sugar syrup or maple syrup if the weather is warm. March can be a month when bees starve, but if you have been feeding since fall they should be fine. More eggs are laid and the first drones appear. Don't stop feeding until the bees are bringing in their own sustenance. Treat the bees for possible Varroa mites.

Bees gather pollen and nectar from Crocus, Witch Hazel and Skunk Cabbage.

April—If there is no brood the queen may be failing. Replace the queen if needed. Keep feeding to stimulate egg laying. More drones are born. On a warm, windless day reverse hive bodies to allow better distribution of brood. Feed the hive with medicated syrup.

Bees gather from Andromeda-Fetterbush, Aspen, Elm, Ash, Beech, Birch, Black Haw, Bloodroot, Box Elder, Cassandra, Dandelion, Deutzia, Gill-Over-The Ground, Hazel, Marsh Marigold, Narcissus, Maple, Shadbush, Spicebush, Alder, Tulips and Willows.

May—Remove dead bees and debris. Nights are still chilly, so keep an entrance reducer on. Inspect for swarm cells that may contain a queen.

Complete spring mite treatments before adding honey supers. Add a queen excluder and watch for swarming or evidence of extra queens. Move extra queens to a new hive.

Bees collect from Apple, Barberry, Beach Plum, Alder, Blueberry, Cherry, Chickweed, Currant, Dogwood, Cranberry, Hobblebush, Honeysuckle, Horse Chestnut, Huckleberry, Crab Apple, Lilac, Mustard, Maple, Pear, Plum, Poppy, Raspberry, Red Oak, Strawberry, Sour Gum, Weigelia, Winged Euonymus and Yellow Rocket.

June—Add a super to the top of the hive or in-between to prevent overcrowding leading to loss of the queen or swarming. Egg laying slows as honey production increases. Keep inspecting for extra queens. Move frames with extra queens to a new hive.

Bees forage for Alfalfa, Clover, Asparagus, Bittersweet, Blackberry, Black Locust, Carrot, Catalpa, Cranberry, Devil's Paintbrush, Elder, Linden, Fox Grape, Hollyhock, Lavender, Lupine, Magnolia, Mignonette, Mint, Privet, Rose, Sage, Snowberry, Sumac, Sweet Mock Orange, Tulip Tree, Vetch and Viper's Bugloss.

July—Keep inspecting the hive. Add supers if necessary (when there is white wax on the edge of the top bars). Keep checking for diseases, loss of the queen or too many drone cells.

Bees forage for Aster, Basswood, Bee Balm, Buckwheat, Butterfly-Bush, Buttonbush, California Poppy, Canada Thistle, Clematis, Corn, Cucumber, Dogbane, Dwarf Sumac, English Ivy, Fireweed, Golden-Rain Tree, Goldenrod, Hardhack,

Marjoram, Meadowsweet, Milkweed, New Jersey Tea, Jewelweed, Onion, Purple Loosestrife, Vervain, Rhubarb, Rock-rose, Smooth Sumac, Swamp Loosestrife, Sweet Pepperbush, Thyme, Wild Cucumber and Winter Squash.

August—Activity slows along with honey flow. No more worries about swarming. Keep an eye out for wasps. Drones are still hanging around.

Bees feed on Bachelor's Button, Boneset, Burdock, Bur-Marigold, Goldenrod, Heart's Ease, Joe-Pye Weed, Ragweed and Virginia Creeper.

September—Drones disappear and hive population shrinks as egg laying slows. Gather honey and set aside sixty pounds per hive for winter. Feed and medicate for mites. Keep feeding. After the first frost place a mouse guard on the hive entrance.

Bees forage for False-Chamomile and Japanese Bamboo.

October—Keep watching for robbing. Install another mouse guard if necessary. Put up a wind break. Keep feeding. Witch Hazel blooms again for the bees.

November/December—Insulate hives with wood chips or leaves in burlap. Add an upper ventilation hole and tack a piece of screen over the main entrance. Make sure no moisture can seep into the hive. Store equipment. Attend a bee club meeting.

–ELLEN EVERT HOPMAN

For beekeepers dealing with a colony collapse, we recommend watching: youtube.com/watch?v=DAw_Zzge49c

DRUMS THAT TALK

The Sacred Rhythms of Yorubaland

THE YORUBA of Southwestern Nigeria have long honored a pantheon of deities (Orisa) that often embody many natural phenomena. They form a spiritual stellium whose domains and qualities intricately weave a rich tapestry of presence in the being of their devotees. While the Orisa to an outsider may seem a disparate group of energies, they inexorably intersect with each other, as well as the spiritual and mundane lives of their followers and priests alike.

Each Orisa cult and its attendant priesthoods are in many ways independent of each other. However, there are certainly points of commonality across the broad array of sects. In the endeavors of each cult divination, sacrifice and herbal knowledge are consistent elements. While the mode and method of the employment of each may vary widely, their use is essential to the livelihood of the constituent cults. The intercession of Ifa and Esu in each of the cults is also paramount.

Another essential element in Orisa worship, as well as Yoruba society collectively, is the use of drums. In Yoruba society the ritual drum is used to bring honor to the family and Orisa alike by way of the recounting of family histories, retelling of the deities' myths and the recitation of praise poetry. The format in which the accompanied voices join with the drums is often a "call and response" singing, with long chants punctuated by the rising and falling of voice and drum alike.

Of Kings and Commoners

The usage of drums in Yorubaland as a whole has remained an essential staple of society and in many instances where the family has moved away from indigenous practices, the usage of the drum has remained constant. The Yorubas to this day continue to maintain the structures of feudal kingship that had been in place prior to the arrival of Europeans and the influx of Christianity and Islam. While the king and his family may have been born outside the native faith of the Orisas, they continue to make use of the drum as a medium of connection to their subjects, as well as a method to recount their "divine" family lineage going back to the Orisa.

Each morning as the sun rises, the king's compound will be filled with the sound of sacred drumming, waking the king. Firstly the drummers will play the traditional oriki (praise poetry) recounting the divine and earthly lineage

of the king. The recounting of the lineage may be accompanied by singers or may simply be through the use of the drums. Yoruba language, like the drums, is tonal. While the human voice may give clarity to the poetry that is being recited, the drum by itself can and does speak in an intelligible manner to those that can understand its language.

The drumming heard from the king's compound is not solely limited to the praises of the king. In many instances it also used as a method of advising the subjects of various problems and situations which the king and his retinue of bureaucrats will encounter for the day. The drums can be heard through the day broadcasting necessary information to the people of the kingdom.

Another common practice within the sovereign's compound is drumming to announce visitors. Each family has their own oriki. On arrival of an important community figure, the drummers will begin to play the oriki of the visitor. This serves to please the "spirits" that guide the family of the visitor, alert the king of the importance of the figure who has just entered his compound and finally alert the community that there is an audience taking place in the compound.

In the case of familial life, drumming is employed by affluent families in much the same way it would in the case of a monarch. Those families that have the means will begin their day with the recitation of family praise poetry and history. This serves

to continue the Yoruba's connection with their past and remembering of the families' prominent members. It also serves as a method of pleasing the ancestral spirits through the singing of their accomplishments. While their history may not be as illustrious as those of the local royal families, they are certainly noteworthy to the individual clans.

Drumming for the sacred

For the Yoruba pantheon, as well as complex religious secret societies, drumming is indispensable. Drumming serves as a means of transmission for the mythology and praise poetry of each individual Orisa, as well as being the backbone of liturgy. Regardless of the ritual mode (regular worship, purification offerings or initiations), it is the drum that guides the liturgy through the narration of the actions or by providing historical context for each of the activities. It is the drummer and the drum, like the priest and diviners they serve, to connect the devotee to the unseen world of the Orisa.

While each Orisa may have a specific type of drum and repertoire of rhythms which are their own, there is a commonality that pervades all liturgical events of each of the cults. All rites must begin with drumming the praise songs of the gate keeper Orisa, Esu. His quirky rhythms that can lead the worshipper in a myriad of directions point to his role as the Orisa representing all possibilities. Through music that is pleasing to Esu, the drummers will cajole this sometimes hot divinity into opening a cool road to ensure the success of the rites to be performed.

Having completed drumming and opening offerings to Esu, the drummers will then proceed to pound out the stately rhythms of Orunmila (also known as Ifa), the messenger of all the divinities and most specifically the divinity in charge of conveying the individuals fate, as well as the will and word of the High God into this world.

After the perfunctory drumming to Esu and Ifa are completed, the drumming can then proceed to drum the liturgy of the task at hand. As already stated, the drums will serve to guide the devotees through the ritual by citing historical precedent of each action vis-à-vis myth or through narration of the acts being performed.

Riding a head like a horse

The central role of most rites, regardless of cult, is to allow the means by which the divinities (as well as ancestors) to manifest in the realm of the devotees. Drumming is a means by which the Orisa are invited, via praise and provocation, to enter into this world. For the most part this manifestation happens by means of possession trance.

The head of each of the initiated priests has been treated with certain medicines at their initiation that spiritually connects them to their Orisa. They in essence become an earthly vehicle that each divinity can ride for a time. Each Orisa has its own origins, personality, taboos and praise poetry. These are all enumerated while entreating the divinity to manifest through one of the initiated priests at each function.

The drums serve to focus the inner head of the devotee, allowing the other priests to guide the Orisa onto the head of the intended priests. As the manifestation becomes increasingly apparent the drummers will take note of the vehicles' demeanor (facial expression and movement of the eyes) and quicken their tempo so as not to allow the Orisa to escape. In some ways, they captivate the divinity — directing it to seat itself on the head of the properly initiated.

The activators within each ritual are the mythical songs, the praise poetry and the rhythms of the drums. They serve to heighten the senses of the active community, quickening a road by which divine energy can manifest in this world. It is the drumming that adds shape to the ceremony, providing a channel for the individual divine energies via their special rhythmic signatures.

While the abode of the Orisa and the spirits (known as Orun) may be separated from the world of the living (known as Aye), the road that connects both is filled with the sound of drums and voices singing praises. The divinities can ride these rhythms into Aye, influencing and guiding their devotees in a very real way before returning to Orun.

Festivals

It is not only through private ritual that drumming is used to invoke the presence of the Orisa. While much activity and drumming will occur in traditional

settings within shrines amongst a tightly knit community, this is not the only setting in which sacred drumming will occur. There are many instances of very public celebrations of the Orisa in which drumming and songs are featured.

Yorubaland has many recurrent public festivals devoted to the various Orisa. Whereas the cults of the Orisa are religious in nature, public festivals celebrate them as the ancestors of a given locality. As is the case of the closed ceremonies of initiates or home shrines, drumming is a prominent constituent element. However, the difference between the public and private rituals can be very marked in as much as the public celebrations of a particular Orisa will have very secular elements to them, with the religious element being at times very minor in nature.

A good example of the difference is the annual Osun Festival held in the city of Osogbo. In this case, the primary reason for the celebration is the establishment of the kingdom by the Orisa Osun. The drummers will assemble to not only beat out the rhythms of Osun, but to accompany the very secular recounting of how this "ancestress" happened upon this spot along the Osogbo river and founded an enclave for humankind. In this case the drummer's repertoire is limited to praises and secular myth rather than inciting the Orisa to take possession of one of her priests.

The secular overtones will be punctuated with an occasional overlapping into religious territory. This excursion back into the spirit realm occurs due to the main officiants of the festival being a mixture of cult priests along with earthly progeny of the Orisa. Using the Osun festival as our example again, while the primary festival leader is the king of Osogbo who is a Muslim, his counterpart is the head priestess of the Osun cult in his principality. The king accepts the offerings on behalf of his ancestress from the hands of the designated virgin. It would be unseemly for an Islamic king to be possessed by the divinity. As such, the drummers will not in the presence of the king incite Osun to mount.

In the case of public activities such as the Osun festival, the rhythms that retell the myths are secular activities with religious overtones used to explore and seek explanation to human origins of a given geographic region and understand its destiny.

The Drum and the Drummer

The drums that are used for ritual purposes are quite different from drums that are used for simple entertainment and secular singing. In fact, the sacred drums used for the worship of a given Orisa are in many cases considered to be alive at the very least and in some instances are in fact recognized as Orisa themselves, albeit subservient the to the Orisa they serve.

For the most part, the making of a drum is an arduous task requiring the harvesting of wood from very specific trees, to which offerings are made prior to the wood being taken. The drum maker will also go through particular cleansing as well before felling a tree. His choice of tree will be based not only on the sacredness of the species, but also on its ability to "speak."

Once all of the requirements are met, both for the drum maker and the tree, then the tree will be felled. Much of the drum making process is a secret not easily shared by drum making guilds. There are processes of herbal baths and certain trigger songs that must be spoken as the drum is fashioned. The strictest of regiments is followed so as not provoke a reaction from the spirit of the drum and the Orisa to which it will play.

Equally important is the training of the drummers. Each Orisa has its drumming class and while drummers may be initiated into the mysteries of a particular Orisa, they most assuredly will be initiated into the mysteries of drumming. This process is not all unlike the initiation into the priesthoods of the various Orisa. The significant difference being that the spirit of the drum does not sit on the head of the drummer, rather it sits on the hands. Orisa priests have medicines put into their scalp, drummers have medicine and lustral baths for their hands.

Like diviners, the drummer must learn by apprenticeship and years of observation. The drumming corpus of each Orisa can be almost as vast as that of learning the poetic corpus each diviner must learn. In addition, the drummer must learn the visual tells of what is happening during worship to the Orisa priests and devotees. They must be able to note subtle differences and decide how to coax the Orisa's manifestation. Also, they must master the ability to make their drum "speak" in the same tonality of language, so that in the absence of a human voice the drum clearly speaks in the Yoruba language.

Drumming the heart

Drums are the glue of Yoruba culture, establishing a transformative relationship between mankind and the Orisa. The vast usage of drums allows for each individual to relate his personal history, his connection to the divine and in a broad sense to the culture that surrounds him. The drums in Yorubaland neatly tie incantation, liturgy, history, myth and cultural identity. May your own drum, your heart, beat out a song that again connects you to the divine.

—Ifadoyin Sangomuyiwa

Orisha says that he says, "A blessing of money;

Orisha says he says, "A blessing of children, a blessing of long life."

"Whether to eat, or to drink

Is a vital matter"

Cast for Bata drum

On the day he was going to be Shango's representative.

There was Shango, and there was Bata;

They were friends, they had been friends from childhood

Shango said, "What should I do so that my friend

will make me wealthy?"

They said an entire bata drum was he should offer as sacrifice.

"What else should I offer?"

They said he should offer 24,000 cowries on the right side;

He should offer 24,000 cowries on the left side:

He should offer two cocks, two pigeons;

They said Shango should go and offer twelve cudgels,

and they gave him one of these cudgels

When he had finished offering the sacrifice,

Excerpt from Ejila Shebora Divination Poem

MOON GARDENING

BY PHASE

| *Sow, transplant, bud and graft* | | *Plow, cultivate, weed and reap* | |

NEW	First Quarter	FULL	Last Quarter	NEW
Plant above-ground crops with outside seeds, flowering annuals.	Plant above-ground crops with inside seeds.	Plant root crops, bulbs, biennials, perennials.		Do not plant.

BY PLACE IN THE ZODIAC

Fruitful Signs

Cancer — Most favorable planting time for all leafy crops bearing fruit above ground. Prune to encourage growth in Cancer.

Scorpio — Second only to Cancer, a Scorpion Moon promises good germination and swift growth. In Scorpio, prune for bud development.

Pisces — Planting in the last of the Watery Triad is especially effective for root growth.

Taurus — The best time to plant root crops is when the Moon is in the sign of the Bull.

Capricorn — The Earthy Goat Moon promotes the growth of rhizomes, bulbs, roots, tubers and stalks. Prune now to strengthen branches.

Libra — Airy Libra may be the least beneficial of the Fruitful Signs, but is excellent for planting flowers and vines.

Barren Signs

Leo — Foremost of the Barren Signs, the Lion Moon is the best time to effectively destroy weeds and pests. Cultivate and till the soil.

Gemini — Harvest in the Airy Twins; gather herbs and roots. Reap when the Moon is in a sign of Air or Fire to assure best storage.

Virgo — Plow, cultivate, and control weeds and pests when the moon is in Virgo.

Sagittarius — Plow and cultivate the soil or harvest under the Archer Moon. Prune now to discourage growth.

Aquarius — This dry sign of Air is perfect for ground cultivation, reaping crops, gathering roots and herbs. It is a good time to destroy weeds and pests.

Aries — Cultivate, weed, and prune to lessen growth. Gather herbs and roots for storage.

Consult our Moon Calendar pages for phase and place in the zodiac circle. The Moon remains in a sign for about two-and-a-half days. Match your gardening activity to the day that follows the Moon's entry into that zodiac sign.

The MOON *Calendar*

is divided into zodiac signs rather than the more familiar Gregorian calendar.

2017

2018

Bear in mind that new projects should be initiated when the Moon is waxing (from dark to full). When the Moon is on the wane (from full to dark), it is a time for storing energy and the wise person waits.

Please note that Moons are listed by day of entry into each sign. Quarters are marked, but as rising and setting times vary from one region to another, it is advisable to check your local newspaper, library or planetarium.
The Moon's Place is computed for Eastern Time.

⚜ Looking Back ⚜

A Thessalian Moon Charm

THESSALY IS A pastoral region in north-eastern Greece long famed as the haunt of witches. Mt. Olympus, abode of the ancient Greek deities, is in Thessaly. So is the site of the inspiring Pierian Spring of the Nine Muses, goddesses of the arts and sciences. Yet Thessaly is primarily renowned for its witches. Their sorcery to draw down the moon has captured the imagination of writers for centuries.

Sophocles and Aristophanes wrote of the Thessalian witches in the fifth century B.C.E. Plato writes of them a century later. Horace, Virgil, Ovid and Lucan hail the moon-drawing charm at the turn of the Christian era. John Dryden in 17th century England described a heroine whose "eyes have power beyond Thessalian charms to draw the moon from heaven."

Today the phrase calls to mind a ceremony performed by contemporary English witches in which the High Priestess becomes the Moon Goddess incarnate. A tape recording of this ritual inspired Margot Adler's study of Neo-Pagans in America and gave her its title: *Drawing Down the Moon.*

But there is another ceremony less well known and similar in theme. We believe this personal and simple rite is probably closer to the original sorcery. Its purpose it to renew psychic energy and increase divinatory perception.

To Draw Down the Moon

At the time of the Full Moon closest to summer solstice and when the Moon is high, go to an open space carrying a small bowl of fresh spring water. Position yourself so as to capture the Moon's reflection in the bowl. Hold it as steadily as you can in both hands for a slow and silent count to nine. Close your eyes and while holding the image of the Moon in your mind, drink the water to the last drop.

– Originally published in the 1991/1992 Witches' Almanac.

capricorn

December 21, 2016 – January 19, 2017
Cardinal Sign of Earth ♁ Ruled by Saturn ♄

S	M	T	W	T	F	S
			Dec. **21** Winter Solstice ❄ Libra	**22** *Praise Mistletoe*	**23** Scorpio	**24** *Observe an old custom*
25 *Little Richard born 1935*	**26** Sagittarius	**27**	**28** *Cast a spell* Capricorn	**29** ●	**30** WAXING	**31** Aquarius
Jan. **1** **2017**	**2** *Weather the storm* Pisces	**3**	**4** Aries	**5** ◑	**6** Taurus	**7** *Plan for the New Year*
8 *Light a candle*	**9** *Feast of Janus* Gemini	**10** *Find your answer*	**11** Cancer	**12** Wolf Moon	**13** WANING Leo	**14** *Surrender to love*
15 Virgo	**16**	**17** *Muhammad Ali born, 1942* Libra	**18** *Bite your tongue*	**19** ◐		

Of Spells: The recitation of spells and charms should be at a tempo much slower than ordinary speech. We are told that the effect should be one of quite emphasis and certain intent. Some say that the sound should be loud and clear; others recommend a whisper. Another source insists that the words be musically intoned.

– ELIZABETH PEPPER, *Magic Spells and Incantations*

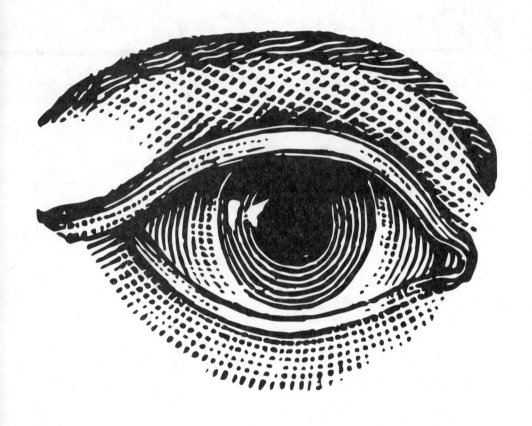

Suddenly I am raised aloft by primordial passion;

I become Leader, Law, Light, Prophet, Father, Author, and Journey.

Rising above this world to the others that shine in their splendor.

I wander through every part of that ethereal country;

Then, far away, as they gape at the marvel, I leave them behind me.
                                            GIORDANO BRUNO (1548–1600)
                                                The Heroic Frenzies

aquarius
January 20 – February 18, 2017
Fixed Sign of Air △ Ruled by Uranus ♅

S	M	T	W	T	F	S
♥	♥	♥	♥	♥	Jan. **20** *Scorpio*	**21**
22 *Scorpio*	**23** *Beware of Jack Frost*	**24** *Louis de wohl born 1903*	**25** *Capricorn*	**26** *Gaze into a black mirror*	**27** ● *Aquarius*	**28** WAXING *Year of the Rooster*
29 WAXING *Pisces*	**30**	**31** *Make an offering*	Feb. **1** *Oimelc Eve* *Aries*	**2** *Candlemas*	**3** ◐ *Taurus*	**4**
5 *Gemini*	**6** *Make an incense*	**7** *Cancer*	**8** *Read the Tarot*	**9** *Partial lunar eclipse* ⇨ *Leo*	**10** ○ *Storm Moon*	**11** WANING *Virgo*
12 *Place silver against gold*	**12**	**14** *Jimmy Hoffa born 1913* *Libra*	**15** *Lupercalia*	**16** *Scorpio*	**17** *Use ginger root*	**18** ◐

Truth: Truth must be loved for its own sake. Those who speak the truth because they are in some way compelled to or for their own advantage, and who are not afraid to tell a lie when it is of no importance to anyone, is not truthful enough. My soul naturally shuns a lie, and hates even the thought of one. I feel an inward shame and a sharp remorse if an untruth happens to escape me — as sometimes it does if the occasion is unexpected, and I am taken unawares. – MICHEL DE MONTAIGNE

The Mystery Fetish of Anubis

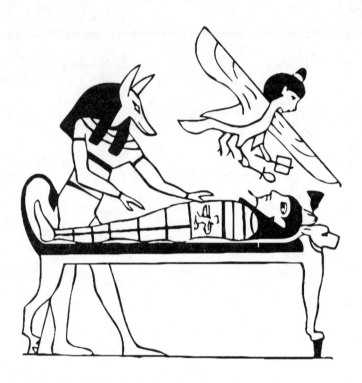

THE GOD ANUBIS is a complex funerary deity, a man's body with the black head of a canine. Jackals and dogs were symbolic of mortality, as the animals tended to hover around cemeteries and scavenge. At the death of an Egyptian, Anubis was on hand to guide the righteous to Osiris, Lord of the Underworld, or to deliver the evildoer to a demon. Mummification, a gift from Anubis, was a long and expensive process, available only to royalty and the elite. Within many tombs a strange fetish, an *imiut*, indicated the protection of Anubis and the promise of eternal life. In the necropolis of Tutankhamen, the fetishes were golden. The imiut form depicted a headless feline tied by its tail to a pole, the stalk of a lotus tipped with a bud, a papyrus flower connecting tail to stalk, and the form planted in a pot. All the golden figures reposed in western corridors of the tomb. Lesser mortals than the pharaoh had the same fetishes in simpler form, real animal skins wrapped in bandages.

The ancient cult of Anubis preceded that of Osiris, and Anubis was preceded by the shadowy god Imiut. This deity was dimly evoked as "He who is in his wrappings," and Imiut eventually merged into the form of Anubis. It is not much of a stretch to link the "wrappings" with the embalming process that we still marvel at down the ages.

– Barbara Stacy

pisces

February 19 – March 20, 2017

Mutable Sign of Water ▽ Ruled by Neptune ♆

S	M	T	W	T	F	S
Feb. **19** Nicholas Copernicus born 1473 Sagittarius	**20**	**21** Capricorn	**22** Call a friend	**23** Aquarius	**24** Eat a sweet	**25**
26 Pisces	**27** WAXING *Partial solar eclipse* ⇦	**28** Aries	Mar. **1** Matronalia	**2** Taurus	**3** Buy seeds	**4** Gemini
5 Cancer	**6** Dream of roses	**7**	**8** Syd Charisses born 1922 Leo	**9**	**10**	**11** Plan your garden Virgo
12 Chaste Moon	**13** WANING Libra	**14**	**15** Meditate on the Moon Scorpio	**16** Search the sky	**17**	**18** Sagittarius
19 Minerva's Day	**20**					

Stronger, Happier, Wiser: No changing of place at a hundred miles an hour will make us one whit stronger, or happier, or wiser. There was always more in the world than we could see, walked we ever so slowly; we will see it no better for going fast. The really precious things are thought and sight, not pace. It does a bullet no good to go fast; and a person, if he or she be truly a man or woman, no harm to go slow; for our glory is not at all in going, but in being.   – JOHN RUSKIN

The Rose and the Amaranth

A ROSE AND AN AMARANTH blossomed side by side in a garden, and the Amaranth said to her neighbor, "How I envy you, your beauty and your sweet scent! No wonder you are such a universal favorite." But the Rose replied with a shade of sadness in her voice, "Ah, my dear friend, I bloom but for a time: my petals soon wither and fall, and then I die. But your flowers never fade, even if they are cut; for they are everlasting."

Moral: Greatness carries its own penalties.

aries

March 21 – April 19, 2017

Cardinal Sign of Fire △ *Ruled by Mars* ♂

S	M	T	W	T	F	S
		Mar. **21** Vernal Equinox Capricorn	**22** Celebrate	**23** Aquarius	**24** Plan your garden	**25** Pisces
26 Enjoy fine dreams	**27** Aries	**28** WAXING	**29**	**30** Taurus	**31** Tease a friend	April **1** April Fools Day Gemini
2	**3** Cancer	**4**	**5** Read the Tarot Leo	**6**	**7** Post to a loved one Virgo	**8**
9 Plant seeds	**10** Cast a spell Libra	**11** Seed Moon	**12** WANING Scorpio	**13** Reveal nothing	**14**	**15** Light a blue candle Sagittarius
16	**17** Knit, weave or braid Capricorn	**18**	**19** Aquarius			

Holed Stone Stones with naturally occuring holes in the center are said to be sacred to the Goddess Diana, the protector of witches. They offer protection and work against black magic and nightmares. Holed stones are thought by some to possess healing properties and are rubbed along the body to absorb disease. Gazing through the hole of such a stone is said to produce visions of spirts.

— Elizabeth Pepper, *The ABC of Magic Charms*

51

TAROT'S WHEEL OF FORTUNE

WHEEL of FORTUNE

THE ROMAN GODDESS FORTUNA held a strong appeal for the late pagan mind. She appears as one of the main characters in Anicius Boethius' popular sixth century work *The Consolation of Philosophy*, and as the deity in charge of fate, was respected by gamblers and fortune-tellers alike. She was renamed Dame Fortune during the Christian Middle Ages, and was feared and propitiated because of her well-known fickleness. The gifts presented at the turn of the year by subjects to their rulers, servants to their masters, were a memory of the old pagan worship. One of her most frequently encountered symbols is a large wheel, the so-called Wheel of Fortune. Illustrations of the Wheel sometimes depict four figures riding it with words emerging from their mouths: *regnabo, regno, regnavi, sum sine regno*: "I will reign, I reign, I have reigned, I am without reign," which tell their own story. Dame Fortune may turn the Wheel herself, blindfolded like Justice to demonstrate just how arbitrary she is. Her Wheel may be considered to represent the questioner's public image, his or her friends and associates, his financial condition or that of his or her employer or business associates. Generally speaking however European cartomancers regard the Wheel as a card of good fortune, growth and prosperity when it appears upright; aggrandizement and the perils deriving therefrom when reversed.

Excerpted from Dame Fortune's Wheel Tarot—A Pictorial Key *by Paul Huson, published by The Witches' Almanac.*

taurus

April 20 – May 20, 2017

Fixed Sign of Earth ♉ Ruled by Venus ♀

S	M	T	W	T	F	S
				April **20**	**21**	**22** *Smile and laugh* Pisces
23	**24** Ares	**25** *Calm your temper*	**26** Taurus	**27** WAXING	**28** *Pray to the stars* Gemini	**29**
30 Walpurgis Night Cancer	May **1** Beltane	**2** Leo	**3**	**4** Virgo	**5** *Foster growth*	**6**
7 *Accept a challenge* Libra	**8**	**9** *Dig in the earth* Scorpio	**10** Hare Moon Vesak Day	**11** WANING	**12** Sagittarius	**13** *Keep your word*
14 Capricorn	**15**	**16** *Avoid risks*	**17** Aquarius	**18**	**19** *Plant more seeds* Pisces	**20**

Fair Wind, ill wind. For sailors, the mood of Aeolus the wind god means everything. He can drown by causing "waves like mountains" or he can protect with a gentle presence that speeds ships to havens. He graced Ulysses, by giving the cleverest of mariners a bag containing unfavorable winds. His crew, curious about the secret of the bag, opened it and released gales that blew the ship back to shore. But Aeolus blew softly to protect his grandchildren.
— ELIZABETH PEPPER, *The ABC of Magic Charms*

A Pagan Manifesto

1. Thou shalt always say, think and do what you truly desire, so long as it hurts no one else.
2. Thou shalt live in accordance with the laws of nature, not against them, and coordinate sleep, food, physical exertion and work with the ways of nature.
3. Thou shalt not destroy nature or take from it without restoring that which has been taken, and thou shalt keep the balance of nature intact at all times.
4. Thou shalt worship in any way that pleases thee and let others do likewise, even though ye may not understand their ways.
5. Thou shalt not take the life of another living thing, except for protection or for food.
6. Thou shalt not cage another living thing.
7. Thou shalt be free to love whomever thou pleasest, so long as thy primary obligations to family, home and community are not neglected.
8. Thou shalt express thyself through art, crafts, music, dancing, singing, poetry, for in so doing, thou shalt be in harmony with nature.
9. Thou shalt accept communication from the world beyond and the inner planes as natural, and thou shalt develop psychic abilities as a natural function of thy personality.
10. Thou shalt always strike a happy balance between mind and body, exercising both and developing thy inner self through the interplay of both selves, ever mindful that the spirit is above and beyond mind and body.
11. Thou shalt not forget the Spirit within and the Spirit without are the one and only true God/dess.

Paganism has one primary law – the law of Threefold Return, which states: Whatever you do, for good or for ill, returns to you threefold.

.

– The New Pagans, HANS HOLZER

gemini

May 21 – June 20, 2017

Mutable Sign of Air ♎ Ruled by Mercury ☿

S	M	T	W	T	F	S
May **21** Aries	**22** Move on Taurus	**23** Read a palm Taurus	**24** Read a palm	**25** ● Gemini	**26** WAXING	**27** Gaze into the heavens Cancer
28	**29** Oak Apple Day Leo	**30**	**31** Cast a spell	June **1** ◑ Virgo	**2**	**3** Libra
4	**5** Night of the Watchers Scorpio	**6** Count clouds	**7**	**8** Chant an incantation Sagittarius	**9** ○ Dyad Moon	**10** WANING Capricorn
11 A healing day	**12**	**13** Hold your tongue Aquarius	**14**	**15** Remember dreams Pisces	**16**	**17** ◐
18 Aries	**19** Gather St. Johnswort	**20** Summer Solstice ☼ Taurus				

Cynthia A name for the Moon Goddess derived from Mount Cynthos on Delos, the birthplace of Artemis and Apollo. Homer tells the story of Leto, a beautiful maiden made pregnant by the sky god Zeus, and how she was denied refuge everywhere for all feared the wrath of Hera, wife of Zeus, who was enraged by his infidelity. Leto was finally granted sanctuary on the desolate isle of Delos where Artemis was safely delivered.

— ELIZABETH PEPPER, *Moon Lore*

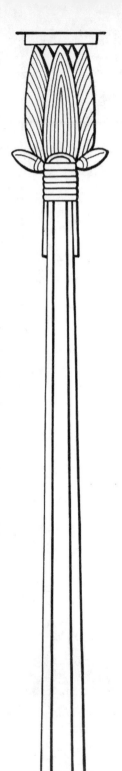
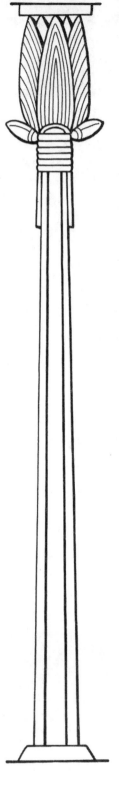

The Blind Priest's Hymn to the Moon

O Moon, sailing up through the sky on high
    Over the Stream of Night,
I beg of thy mercy a boon, O Moon,
    Grant me to see thy light.

Once I took falsely, O shame! his name,
    He smote me with his might.
I gazed all around and saw with awe,
    Darkness at noonday's height.

O people of Egypt, I call to all,
    Fear ye the God of Night!
Bow ye your heads in his rays, and praise
    The Lord of Truth and Right.

I tell all the birds of the air, Beware,
    Ware of the Moon's great might;
I tell all the fish of the deep, who sleep
    Safe in his holy light.

O Moon, sailing up through the sky on high
    Where darkly flows the Night!
Of thy mercy a boon, O Lord adored,
    Give me again my sight.

Translated from the original in
Egyptian Poems *by Margaret Murray*

cancer
June 21 – July 22, 2017
Cardinal Sign of Water ▽ Ruled by Moon ☽

CANCER

S	M	T	W	T	F	S
			June 21	22 Brew tea Gemini	23	24 Midsummer WAXING Cancer
25	26 Postpone decisions Leo	27	28 Virgo	29	30 Libra	July 1 Defeat a curse
2	3 Spend this day alone Scorpio	4	5 Sagittarius	6 Avoid fire	7	8 Capricorn
9 Mead Moon	10 WANING Aquarius	11 Water flows	12	13 Travel over water Pisces	14	15 Aries
16	17 Taurus	18	19 Whistle Gemini	20	21 Bake cookies Cancer	22

To Draw Down the Moon At the time of the Full Moon closest to Summer Solstice when the Moon is high, go to an open space carrying a small bowl of fresh spring water. Position yourself so as to capture the Moon's reflection in the bowl. Hold it as steady as you can in both hands for a slow and silent count of nine. Close your eyes and while holding the Moon's image in your mind drink the water to the last drop.

– THE WITCHES' ALMANAC, *Love Charms*

Ægishjálmr

The Helm of Awe

THE ÆGISHJÁLM or the Helm of Awe is an offensive rune meant to impart protection and assure victory.

In both *The Galdrabók* (the Icelandic Book of Magic) and the *Fáfnismál* (an Eddic poem) the Helm of Awe is used to overpower enemies.

It is Frænir, the dragon son of the Dwarf King Hreidmar, who uses of the Helm of Awe to remain invincible:

The Helm of Awe
I wore before the sons of men
In defense of my treasure;
Amongst all, I alone was strong, I
thought to myself,

For I found no power a match for
  my own

The Galdrabók provides a spell appropriately named "Simple Helm of Awe Working" to use:

Make a helm of awe in lead, press the lead sign between the eyebrows, and speak the formula:

Ægishjálm er ég ber
milli brúna mér!

I bear the helm of awe
between my brows!

In a time of need, to use the Helm of Awe, one need only make the symbol and press it between your brows. If you are out in public or at work, simply project it from your third eye.

–DEVON STRONG

58

leo

July 23 – August 22, 2017

Fixed Sign of Fire △ Ruled by Sun ☉

S	M	T	W	T	F	S
July **23** ● Leo	**24** Ancient Egyptian New Year ⇦	**25** WAXING Virgo	**26**	**27** Libra	**28** *Daydream*	July **29**
30 ◗ Scorpio	**31** Lughnassad Eve	Aug. **1** Lammas Sagittarius	**2**	**3** *Bake bread*	**4** Capricorn	**5**
6 *Sacrifice your feelings* Aquarius	**7** (Wort Moon)	**8** Partial Lunar Eclipse ⇦	**9** WANING Pisces	**10**	**11** Aries	**12** *Don't be angry*
13 *Diana's Day* Taurus	**14** ◖	**15** Gemini	**16** *Feed the birds*	**17** Black Cat Appreciation Day Cancer	**18**	**19** *Dance*
20 *Watch sunrise* Leo	**21** ●	**22** Total Solar Eclipse ⇦ Virgo				

Vesta In the round one-room huts of neolithic Italy, the hearth occupied the center. Here the family gathered for warmth and food, and the same life-substaining site served as the household altar. Before each meal the family offered scraps of food in a little bowl to Vesta, the Numen, the divine spirit of the hearth fire.
— BARBARA STACY, *Ancient Roman Holidays*

Goat Song

SINCE THE DAWN of time, the goat has held divine significance in many cultures. The sacred robes of Babylonian priests were made of goatskins. The zodiacal Capricorn with head and body of a goat and a fish's tail, was established as early as the 15th century B.C.E.; the Sea Goat appears engraved on gems dated to the height of Chaldean rule in Babylon. A cuneiform inscription calls the goat "sacred and exalted,"—and at that time this sign was designated as the "Father of Light." Despite the glory the goat enjoyed among the ancients, its present reputation as a symbol of lust and evil is due to the devil-lore devised by medieval churchmen.

Perhaps the goat's character as loathsome and unclean began when the early Hebrews chose it as the animal to carry away the sins of the community in an annual rite of atonement. The hapless scapegoat was driven into the wilderness to perish bearing all the blame for crimes committed by others.

How wildly different is the ancient Greek symbolism regarding the same animal. Associated with the Gods Dionysus and Pan, the goat represent the pure, spontaneous joy of being alive. The great god Zeus was nurtured by the she-goat Amalthea. Her name is given to the mythical Horn of Plenty, the cornucopia promising its possessor an abundance of all things desired.

We owe the art of drama to the music and dance celebrations honoring Dionysus. The goat and the god were one—the essence of high spirits and joyful abandon. The chorus and dancers wore goatskins and the rites were performed in an orderly manner until a singer named Thespis broke the rules and began a dispute with the choral leader. His action established dialogue and ever after the religious rituals were plays, for the unexpected is in the very nature of the god himself. Thespian became another word for actor. The highest form of drama, the tragedy, means goat song in Greek.

In northern Europe, the goat was revered for its playful nature, a nature firmly ruled by discipline. The love goddess of Germanic tribes rode a goat to the May Eve revels. She held an apple to her lips, a hound and a hare ran beside her and a raven flew overhead. Thor, the red-headed Norse god of thunder, drove a chariot drawn by two fierce goats. Both god and goddess were in complete control of their animals.

The Greeks warn us that when we deny the wildness in human nature, we court disaster. The message from the North is just as wise: we should acknowledge the wildness, use it to advantage, and learn to temper its force with strength and understanding.

virgo

August 23 – September 22, 2017

Mutable Sign of Earth ♍ Ruled by Mercury ☿

S	M	T	W	T	F	S
			Aug. **23** WAXING	**24** Libra	**25** *Take flight* Ganesh Festival	**26** Scorpio
27	**28** *Call a griffin*	**29** Sagittarius	**30**	**31** *Remain safely indoors* Capricorn	Sept. **1**	**2**
3 *Burn incense* Aquarius	**4**	**5** Pisces	**6** Barley Moon	**7** WANING Aries	**8**	**9** *Count flower petals* Taurus
10	**11**	**12** *Call a friend* Gemini	**13**	**14** *Bury an offering in the earth* Cancer	**15**	**16** *Bless a familiar* Leo
17 *Brew tea*	**18** Virgo	**19** *Scry after sunset*	**20** Libra	**21** WAXING	**22** *Plan a party*	

Trivia The word may now be synonymous with worthless knowledge, but in times gone by it was the name Romans gave Hecate. Her triple-form statues stood where three roads met and so they called her Trivia—tri, three and via, road. The crossroads, sacred to the dark goddess, suggest moments of decision.

– ELIZABETH PEPPER, *Moon Lore*

THO, AS HER MANNER WAS ON SUNNY DAY,
DIANA, WITH HER NYMPHES ABOUT HER DREW
TO THIS SWEET SPRING; WHERE, DOFFING HER ARRAY
SHE BATHÈD HER LOVELY LIMBS, FOR IOVE A
                    LIKELY PRAY.

·M· VI· XLV·

Diana and her nymphs
From Walter Crane's illustrations of *The Faerie Queene*

libra

September 23 – October 22, 2017

Cardinal Sign of Air ♎ *Ruled by Venus* ♀

LIBRA

S	M	T	W	T	F	S
			Utchat The Eye of Hours is one of the most common Egyptian amulets. It gives the wearer health, strength, protection and the vigor of the life-giving sun. There are two versions of this symbol—one facing right, one facing left—and are CONTINUED BELOW			Sept. **23** Autumnal Equinox ♌
24 *Gather acorns*	**25** Sagittarius	**26**	**27** 🌓	**28** *Gather fall leaves* Capricorn	**29**	**30** Aquarius
Oct. **1**	**2** *Ask no questions* Pisces	**3**	**4** *Fly to the Circle*	**5** Blood Moon Aries	**6** WANING	**7** *Walk the woods* Taurus
8 *Gather acorns*	**9** Gemini	**10** *Strong winds blow*	**11** Cancer	**12** 🌗	**13** Leo	**14** *Read a book*
15 Virgo	**16** *Keep your mystery*	**17** Libra	**18** *Tell ghost stories*	**19** ●	**20** WAXING Scorpio	**21**
22 Sagittarius	sometimes called the Eye of Ra or the Eye of Horus, with one representing the Sun, the other the Moon. The Book of the Dead says these amulets should be made from lapis lazuli, though many are made from gemstones or metals. The utchat was placed with the deceased or painted on an object for protection. – ELIZABETH PEPPER, *The ABC of Magic Charms*					

The Witches' Sabbat
Vintage postcard

scorpio

October 23 – November 21, 2017
Fixed Sign of Water ▽ Ruled by Pluto ♀

SCORPIVS

S	M	T	W	T	F	S
	Oct. **23**	**24** *Avoid the hungry dead*	**25** Capricorn	**26**	**27** Aquarius	**28** *Prepare the feast*
29	**30** *Honor the dead* Pisces	**31** Samhain Eve	Nov. **1** Hallowmas Aries	**2**	**3** *Visit a cemetery* Taurus	**4** Snow Moon
5 WANING Gemini	**6** *Honor the twins*	**7** *Gaze into a crystal* Cancer	**8**	**9** *Gather fall leaves* Leo	**10**	**11** Virgo
12	**13** *Court the garnet stone*	**14** Libra	**15** *Place an offering at the crossroads*	**16** Hecate Night Scorpio	**17** Saturnalia	**18**
19 WAXING Sagittarius	**20** *Close the veil*	**21** Capricorn				

Pearl Beneficial, protective and akin to the Moon, the pearl represents the soul and the mystic center of the personality. It was the favorite jewel of the goddess Venus, and accordingly the ancient Romans wore pearls in their hair to ensure romantic success and disolved the stone for use in love potions. Moslems and Christians have associated the pearl with heaven. Chinese tradition holds that it is symbolizes "genius in obscurity."
— ELIZABETH PEPPER, *The ABC of Magic Charms*

A DAY AT THE RACES

THE PLEASURE-MAD ROMANS were such avid race fans that they screamed their way through eight annual events. The First Equirra fell on February 27 and the 260,000 seats of the Circus Maximus were packed. Aristocrats occupied the lower marble seats, plebeians sat on wooden tiers above the races. Proceedings began with an homage to Mars, the god of war and horses; the superbly trained animals considered auxiliaries of Rome's military might. The track was so tightly rounded that immense skill was required to prevent being flung onto the track at each turn. The charioteers were often slaves, held in high regard for their mastery of the sport. Preliminary celebration began with a parade of carts holding images of the gods, followed by acrobats, clowns, a rowdy brass band. Then the presiding official threw a white flag on the track and chariots were off, sparks shooting from wheels, whizzing the track, spilling the daredevil drivers. Rousing fans to frenzies.

—BARBARA STACY

sagittarius

November 22 – December 20, 2017

Mutable Sign of Fire △ Ruled by Jupiter ♃

S	M	T	W	T	F	S
			Nov. **22** *Cleanse your home*	**23**	**24** Aquarius	**25**
26 ◗ Pisces	**27**	**28** Aries	**29** *Tell a story*	**30**	Dec. **1** *Toss a coin for luck* Taurus	**2**
3 ◖Oak Moon Gemini	**4** WANING	**5** Cancer	**6** *Share photos with a friend*	**7** Leo	**8** *Praise art*	**9** Virgo
10 ◗	**11** Libra	**12** *Make a spicy incense*	**13** *Light candles* Scorpio	**14**	**15**	**16** *Sing!* Sagittarius
17 Fairy Queen Day	**18** ● Capricorn	**19** WAXING	**20**	*JULLBUCK*: Jullbuck is a Swedish charm made of straw in the form of a goat. The amulet stands about six inches high and is used for sympathetic magic to ensure good crops.		

The goat has an additional magical significance in that part of the world. According to Scandinavian myth, the goat Heidrum provided intoxicating liquor for those heroes slain in battle and magically transported them to the warm and brightly lighted hall of Valhalla where they enjoyed a pleasure-filled afterlife.

– The Witches' Almanac, *Magic Charms from A to Z*

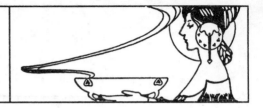

Glögg

GLÖGG, ALSO KNOWN as Svařené Víno in the Czech Republic, Glühwein in Germany and mulled wine in English speaking countries, is a customary drink of Sweden. It is traditionally enjoyed on St. Lucia's Day, a holiday that celebrates light over darkness. Evergreen trees and holly decorate homes as they maintain ancient Pagan traditions by representing life everlasting during the cold dark holiday season.

Historically, it was considered ill-fated for a visitor to leave a Swedish household during the holiday season without offering the guest some form of refreshment—usually Glögg. As a staple drink throughout the Yuletide season, it is generally enjoyed from December 13 through the Winter Solstice.

Every winter my Swedish grandmother would make Glögg (pronounced glerg)—a wonderful, traditional Nordic drink. It was usually served during the cold winter holidays to warm you, bring good fortune and cheer for the coming year. This recipe was handed down from my grandmother to my older brother and eventually to me.

To make Swedish Glögg:
¼ cup vodka
1 quart apple juice or cider
3 whole cloves
2 cups of dry red wine
3 cups water
2 cinnamon sticks or ½ tsp ground cinnamon
½ tsp ground cardamom
½ to ¾ cups of raisins or dried cranberries.

Bring all ingredients to a simmer for 20 minutes

Add small hand-full of raisins or cranberries to each serving cup.

Serve with gingerbread.

This will take the bite off a cold winter's night—enjoy!

–THOR VOLKER

capricorn

December 21 2017 – January 19, 2018
Cardinal Sign of Earth ▽ Ruled by Saturn ♄

S	M	T	W	T	F	S
				Dec. **21** Winter Solstice ❄ Aquarius	**22** *Kiss the mistletoe*	**23** Pisces
24 *Listen to your familiar*	**25**	**26** ◑ Aries	**27** *Set a fire of oak*	**28** Taurus	**29**	**30** Gemini
31 *Summon Jack Frost*	Jan. **1** Wolf Moon Cancer	**2** WANING	**3** Leo	**4** *Family day*	**5** Virgo	**6** *Stir the cauldron*
7 Libra	**8** ◑	**9** *Hold hands with your love*	**10** Scorpio	**11** *Weather the storm*	**12** Sagittarius	**13** *Look to the North*
14 *Build a snowman*	**15** Capricorn	**16** ●	**17** WAXING Aquarius	**18**	**19** *Make a wish*	

Water of Well-Being Go to the seashore after the tide turns from ebb to flood. Collect from the ninth wave a jar of sea water. The count begins at your discretion. It can be the first wave to touch your feet or a breaking crest you see at a distance. Counting the waves by sight is often confused by contrary currents or eddies, so it is far easier to close your eyes and depend on the sound of each wave as it hits the shore. Scoop up water from the ninth wave in one fluid motion.
– THE WITCHES' ALMANAC, *Love Charms*

YEAR OF THE FIRE ROOSTER
January 28, 2017–February 15, 2018

THE CHINESE ZODIAC is among the oldest of the world's calendars. Based upon a twelve-year cycle, it is followed throughout the Orient. There are several traditions concerning its precise origin, but the gist of it is that when Buddha was about to leave the Earth he invited the animals to say farewell. The twelve who came were each rewarded with a year. Buddha decreed that they would be the animals to hide within the events of the year as well as inside the hearts of those born that year. Five elements (fire, water, metal, earth, and wood) are also a part of the system. Every sixty years the animal and element combinations will repeat. Chinese New Year is celebrated at midnight (in China) on the second New Moon after the Winter Solstice. This date varies from year to year, taking place between late January and mid-February.

2017 is the Year of the Fire Rooster. This is a cocky, flashy and bossy bird with an attitude. The general mood is enthusiastic, brave, tenacious and adventurous. The conspicuous rooster is proud of its fine feathers. This is a year to dress exceptionally well. Remember, this straightforward bird is a leader, arising early to welcome the dawn with his loud crowing. Loyalty, a strong work ethic, communication skills and superlatives of all kinds will lead to success. Focus on nonconformity, cultivating new friends, quality and a zest for creative expression. At the same time there is a tendency to be overly impulsive. Analyze the pros and cons of any financial risk before flying the coop to enter uncharted territory.

Those born in years of the Rooster can expect to realize a long cherished dream. The mood is relaxed and life is orderly.

More information on the Fire Rooster can be found on our website at http://The WitchesAlmanac.com/AlmanacExtras/.

Years of the Rooster
1933, 1945, 1957, 1969, 1993, 2005, 2017

Illustration by Ogmios MacMerlin

aquarius

January 21 – February 18, 2018

Fixed Sign of Air ♎ Ruled by Uranus ♅

S	M	T	W	T	F	S
Diana of Ephesus Evolved from a date-palm tree sacred to the Amazons, the well-known statue of Diana is decorated with a festoon of ripe dates. Historical sources mistakenly identify the dates as breasts and dismiss the primary significance of the figure. The statue is a tribute to the tender regard held by Diana for both wild and domestic creatures. From waist to feet are carvings of rows of animals—lions, rams, bulls and deer. Cats climb to her shoulders and an ancient reference CONTINUED BELOW						Jan. **20** Pisces
21 *Write a letter*	**22** Aries	**23**	**24** ◐ Taurus	**25**	**26** *Drop the sail* Gemini	**27**
28 *Ring a bell* Cancer	**29**	**30** Total Lunar Eclipse Blue Moon ⇨	**31** Storm Moon Leo	Feb. **1** WANING Oimelc Eve	**2** Candlemas Virgo	**3** *The kiss fades*
4 *Read tea leaves* Libra	**5**	**6** *Bewitch a stranger* Scorpio	**7** ◐	**8** Sagittarius	**9** *Burn a candle for love*	**10**
11 Capricorn	**12**	**13** *A love found* Aquarius	**14** Lupercalia Partial Solar Eclipse ⇨	**15** ●	**16** Chinese New Year Earth Dog Pisces	**17** WAXING
18 Aries	notes the crab engraved on her breast, "a creature sacred to her." Upon the original statue, the one destroyed by a Christian zealot in A.D. 400, a mysterious inscription appeared in three places: at her feet, girdle and crown. ASKI. KATASKI. HAIX. TETRAZ. DAMNAMENEUS. AISION translated as follows: Darkness-Light-Himself-The Sun-Truth. — ELIZABETH PEPPER, *Moon Lore*					

Notable Quotations

WATER

There is no small pleasure in sweet water. [Lat., *Est in aqua dulci non invidiosa voluptas.*]
Ovid
Epistoloe Ex Ponto

All water is off on a journey unless it's in the sea, and it's homesick, and bound to make its way home someday
Zora Neale Hurston Quotes

Water which is too pure has no fish
Afghan Proverb

Water its living strength first shows, When obstacles its course oppose.
Johann Wolfgang von Goethe
God, Soul, and World—Rhymed Distichs

The miller sees not all the water that goes by his mill.
Robert Burton
Anatomy of Melancholy

Water is the mother of the vine, The nurse and fountain of fecundity, The adorner and refresher of the world.
Charles Mackay
The Dionysia

It is the calm and silent water that drowns a man.
Ghanaian Proverb

Till taught by pain, Men really know not what good water's worth; If you had been in Turkey or in Spain, Or with a famish'd boat's-crew had your berth, Or in the desert heard the camel's bell, You'd wish yourself where Truth is—in a well.

Lord Byron
Don Juan

Quotes compiled by Isabel Kunkle.

pisces

February 19 – March 20, 2018

Mutable Sign of Water ▽ Ruled by Neptune ♆

S	M	T	W	T	F	S
	Feb. **19** Start early	**20**	**21** Break the ice Taurus	**22**	**23** 🌓 Gemini	**24**
25 Bide your time Cancer	**26**	**27** Remove an obstacle Leo	**28** Matronalia ⇨	Mar. **1** Chaste Moon Virgo	**2** WANING	**3** Renounce bigotry Libra
4 Call an old friend	**5** Scorpio	**6**	**7** Intensify efforts	**8** Sagittarius	**9** 🌗	**10** Capricorn
11 Lighten your burden	**12**	**13** Enjoy whimsy Aquarius	**14** Put your house in order	**15** Pisces	**16** Wake the earth	**17** ⚫ Aries
18 WAXING	**19** Minerva's Day	**20** Taurus				

Rhodonite A pink stone with black veining, usually found as a massive single stone; sometimes smaller crystals are found, rare and more valuable. The name "rhodonite" is derived from the Greek "rhodon," meaning "rose." Typically this stone is found in Europe and Australia, but sometimes emerges elsewhere in the world.

Rhodonite is a stone of love and often this sentiment is manifest in self actualization. The earthly gem helps to stabilize emotions, which provides confidence and allows wearers to achieve their full potential. Often helpful in friendships, relationships and negotiating, rhodonite would do well placed in a desk drawer or near the threshold of your front door.

– ELIZABETH PEPPER, *The ABC of Magic Charms*

The Witch and the Devil

IN TAKING THE WITCH as prototype for a modern personal identity, people have taken many historical liberties and forged new paths for themselves. This is good. It is also possibly unavoidable, since the Witch, as opposed to the priestess or folk-healer, is more mythical than historical and always was. Historicity was never the principle factor.

Historical magicians tended to be male, and at least educated if not outright elite. The Witch existed mainly in belief, certainly as a literary trope, but also more widely. She was female, probably lower class—or outcast vulgar and libidinous. She was, of course, a demonized figure. Also, lest we forget, largely mythic rather than historic; though doubtless you could get some serious folk magic done by actual women.

Fortunately, the Romans weren't big on witch-hunts; they just had laws against curses and such, and didn't blink when the defendants were generally the aforesaid literate males. Further back in time, early Middle Eastern magic archived its official tenets and described the 'witchcraft' they were combating in the process. Archaeologists have dug up these archives and have dug up evidence of magic countering witchcraft. What they haven't found is evidence of actual witchcraft. Again, the Witch is more a mythical figure, and even when we're dealing with historical cults & practices, the mythic component is inseparable from it. She existed first and foremost as a coherent mythological type; the concept or its components were part of popular belief. Like God, if she didn't exist she would have had to be invented.

The mythological intimacy of the Witch and the Devil (himself a demonized figure) is all embracing. Some Heathen or Neopagan practitioners, in the process of defining 'witch' for themselves, have found no use for the Devil. The individual in

such cases is a prototypical modern practitioner, the devil a figure from an alien theology. However, when we understand the term "witch" to indicate a pre-existing mythical figure, there is every reason to object to the separation.

Also, if we attempt to reclaim magic, excluding both witch and devil, it is almost equally difficult. Even looking at learned magic performed by solo magicians, apparently distinct from witchcraft as such, she—and the Horned One—are still there. The idea of pacts with dark and mysterious forces was associated with witches and wizards well before it appeared in the grimoires. The modern magician is in fact dependent on the mythical Witch, and of course devils, at every turn. This is illustrated in the story of an adept finding a book by the magician Saint Cyprian.

I found it among others of different species, in the small bookstore of a village priest. It was written in German, a language completely unintelligible to me. However, by some figures in the text and by some names sprinkled here and there, I deduced that the strange opuscule dealt with Magic. A learned scholar translated it lucidly, undertaking his work with extreme scrupulousness. On reading the translation, I saw that this small book is really most notable. Composed by the German monk Jonas Sufurino; the librarian of the monastery on the Brocken —that mountain where, according to old legend, the devils and sorceresses celebrated his Sabbats and the dance macabre—turned out to be a treasure of True Magic.

The Sabbatic goat was sometimes referred to as Leonard, and also features in grimoires. For instance in the Magical Elements of Saint Cyprian, among the chief spirits listed:

Léonard presides over Sabbats under the dark figure of a black goat.

This is of course the most important demon at the Sabbat, the one in the middle, but not the only one. Also, this spirit's appearance incidentally is identical to Lucifuge Rofocale of the Grand Grimoire. So even ceremonial magic needed both witch and devil, and probably still does. At the same time however, while witch and devil can do without ceremonial magic, they are themselves inseparable.

Insofar as modern witchcraft is either European or frequently takes European or Scandinavian models, the Medieval Witch —mythical or otherwise—is of central importance. Folk belief, be it Christian or otherwise involves the language of myth as well. Thus, in understanding The Witch, the mythic figure is primary—excluding the Devil can only render it incomprehensible. We are, consciously or otherwise, reconstructing the Witch, and her relations with the Devil are a part of her. Thus when—so to speak—we invoke her, the Horned One comes along as part of the package. Besides, if you're going to dance back to back at the Sabbat, it isn't half as much fun dancing by yourself.

—JAKE STRATTON-KENT

Sweet Madness
One Honey of a Mysterious Tale

THE ROMAN SOLDIERS must have been surprised and delighted by the welcoming gift they received from the locals when General Pompey led an invasion along the Black Sea in 67 B.C.E. Today more well-intentioned visitors and tourists take the same journey, tantalized by a quest. The soldiers were hailed with friendly waves and smiles and presented with a gift of pretty combs of sweet, dripping honey. The unsuspecting and battle weary invaders began to bite and swallow huge chunks of the unexpected treat. They met with one of the most effective and clever weapons of mass destruction of all time. It was *deli bal*, or mad honey.

Different gourmet honeys, produced by the pollination of bees from an array of plants, fruits and wildflowers, are widely sought for various curative and culinary properties. Health food aficionados might claim that some honeys relieve allergies, hormonal problems, infections or other ailments. A master chef might insist that a particular honey is the secret ingredient needed to prepare a special sauce. However few are aware that one certain honey has the potential to destroy as well as delight, all within seconds of tasting a mere spoonful. One recent visitor cautiously purchased some deli bal from a shopkeeper in the only place in the world where it can be found, a remote region of Turkey. Upon placing a mere few drops on his tongue he reported his mouth immediately grew numb. Locals call it bitter honey and recognize it by the burning sensation it will cause to the touch.

Deli bal has a rich and intriguing history. Since at least the 1700s it has been sought by those who want

the ultimate high. Completely legal, it is only regulated by those who surreptitiously offer it for sale, usually from frothy crocks tucked out of sight in hard to find shops. Those who seek deli bal must travel to the mountainous regions bordering the Black Sea and ask around. Begin in the town of Trabzon or in the Turkish province of the same name.

In tiny amounts, usually taken at breakfast time boiled with milk, deli bal is said to induce lovely sensations including visions, hallucinations and finally a peaceful stupor. Swallowed with a sip of alcohol the sweet syrup might create a head spinning sensation bringing a more intense experience. In larger amounts, for example spread on toast as a regular honey might be served, deli bal disorients, intoxicates and paralyzes. Mad honey can even bring death. History tells us the unfortunate Roman soldiers collapsed with nausea, hallucinations and convulsions. They were then easily slain by the locals loyal to King Mithridates.

Despite, or perhaps because of, its legendary effects this very rare and dubious treat, deli bal, has been treasured over the centuries. Sometimes dubbed "rose of the forest honey" honoring its dark red color, it is produced when bees pollinate with just three of the seven hundred or so species of the rhododendron flower. The rain drenched mountain slopes near the Black Sea provide the perfect habitat for these flowers to flourish. The obliging beekeepers drag their hives to remote fields where the plants are isolated. This is done so that other nectars won't get mixed in, creating an adulterated honey. It is said that the first honey produced by the bees in the early spring is the most potent.

A scientist, Dr. Suleyman Turedi of the University of Karadeniz School of Medicine, has determined the substance grayanotoxin is the active ingredient found in these few varieties of rhododendron flowers from which deli bal is produced. Dr. Turedi claims to have witnessed at least 200 cases of mad honey poisoning while doing his research. Nevertheless, deli bal does have a loyal following among those who claim to benefit from ingesting it. Some insist that it will cure high blood pressure, diabetes and stomach problems. The beekeepers of Trabzon profit nicely from their efforts. Although deli bal has been offered for sale over the Internet caution is advised. It is probably not the pure product and can cost hundreds of dollars a pound. Those who offer genuine mad honey for sale honor its mysterious powers and are cautious. They prefer to deal directly only with those in the know.

—ELAINE NEUMEIER

$\bigcap$ RT $\bigcap$ S $\bigcap$ AGICK

ART MAY BE ONE of the oldest, most ancient forms of magick. Whether our ancestors made cave paintings to influence their hunting, tell stories or adorn their living space, the practice speaks of both artistry and intent—harkening back thousands upon thousands of years to the dawn of civilization.

Divine Expression

Humankind creates to express itself. Music, dance, visual arts and theater all serve to relate the mystery and reality of our existence. Through art we give form to the divine, share our personal and cultural stories, interact with our environment and each other. Therefore art is a primary form of communication, whether we are using it to commemorate an occasion or person, to explore a concept or mystery, to bring social awareness or to build or decorate the living space around us.

Spellcraft is also a vehicle of communication. Through it, we focus our intentions to influence the world around us, create new forms and patterns, and appeal to or align with deities and spirits. A votive candle gives form to will through color, smell, the activation of burning and may include imagery to harness that intent. A poppet is crafted to take on the likeness of a person or animal to affect the subject sympathetically or act as an intermediary. An offering of curated items could be used to appease, honor or invoke a deity or ancestor. Truly,

it is the process of creation combined with the harnessing of will that creates magick beyond the sum of the parts used.

So how do we consciously combine art and magick?

Willing Infinity

In math class, we are taught that a line is a connection of dots that continues to infinity in both directions. If we consider the line as a stand-in for atoms and molecules, we start to have an inkling of its power and how it can bend and change with will.

Throughout the world, "simple" line drawings are used for magick. Consider the *veves* of Vodou practice which are specific line drawings used to summon/invoke a *Lwa* or *Loa*. How did this come to be? If you could not own anything,

if you could not make statues of your deities, nor leave evidence of your practice without fear of punishment or death, then the line that can be drawn temporarily to honor the spirits becomes a mighty thing. In aboriginal culture, collections of lines and dots represent the lay of the land, the way of the gods, and the experiences of the Dreamtime. In Berber tribes, linear tattoos not only marked one's tribe and heritage but also protected both body and spirit. In Western Ceremonial Magic traditions, sigils are used to summon and banish spirits, to protect and to conjure. All are very different markings with distinct purposes, yet are brought together by the power of intent behind them.

Whether a line is drawn as a specific mark or used to channel spirits or energy through automatic writing, scientific studies have shown there is a powerful link between the drawn line and our memory. The drawn line greatly improves our memory and could very likely improve the focus of our magickal intent.

Eclectic Textures

Once we go past the simplicity of line, we begin to add other elements — the more complex application of color, texture and media. A painting not only represents a person or deity but can also create atmosphere, summon a location, embellish a memory and act as a portal.

Each color that is used, every material or item included can add another layer of meaning to the final piece, even if it's not visible in the finished product. Consider what colors have special meaning for you and how they make you feel. What does it mean to paint on canvas, leather, stone or paper? What about adding crushed herbs, candle wax, hair or thread? The possibilities are endless once you begin to think about it!

Molding Intent

While paintings can transform two-dimensional space in magickal ways, sculpture and hand-crafted objects seem to embody spiritual energy even more so. Whether it's the uncanny valley effect of human-shaped sculpture representing the gods, ourselves as votives or poppets, or a vessel crafted to contain a spirit or sacrament, the inanimate object has long held a special fascination for mankind. We can touch it, hold it, see ourselves in it and recognize the hand that has crafted it even if it is not our own. As time and generations pass the object along it can collect even more energy.

The choice of sculptural medium can also bring a lot of meaning to a piece beyond its representational form. Carving wood or stone, building wax or clay, weaving fabric, working glass and forging metal all evoke specific elements, giving form to things we can relate to. Perhaps because it often takes much practice, concentration and skill to work with these materials successfully, they become imbued with so much thought and power in the process.

Renewed Vision

Consider the art and artful objects around you with a fresh eye. How do they influence your daily and spiritual life? What memories and emotions do they embody and how does that add to your life? Whether you collect and curate the art of others or make your own, consider the power it may contain to transform and inspire. It will connect you to a long magickal history!

–LAURA TEMPEST ZARKOFF

Window on the Weather

Since the dawn of time, humankind has pursued the knowledge of things to come with vehemence only matched by the species' will to survive and perpetuate in its time on this green earth. The pursuit to know the right time to conceive, marry, conquer, travel and sow has been over-riding. Some of the methods employed in these very important pursuits have been esoteric, as well as scientific. Our need to discern future weather conditions has not been exempt from our need to know.

The prediction of weather has moved from the domain of the priest-seer to the domain of the meteorological scientist relying on the review of past data and multiple variables in the present in order to glimpse conditions of the future. While looking into the weather for tomorrow or next week can be a laborious task, forecasting a year can be wrought with intricacies that are complex beyond the imagination.

Meteorologists use many tools to tackle long-term weather forecasting. In creating this *Window on the Weather*, our meteorologist Tom Lang, considers orientation of the earth in its orbit, the irregular shape of orbit, cosmic disturbances such as Sun spots, interstellar radiation and human activity, along with a myriad of other variables that will influence trends for 2017.

SPRING

MARCH 2017. Cooling Pacific Ocean water temperatures are likely to bring relatively dry conditions to North America. West Coast rain and snow will persist however with more short-term drought relief. Snowfall will also persist throughout the inter-mountain West with below normal temperatures. In the Southeast, warm and dry weather can be expected with the risk of brush fires running high in Florida. Mild weather will extend through the Mid-Atlantic. From the Ohio Valley to New England, several late season snowfalls can be expected, punctuating a cold and snowy winter. The Great Plains will enjoy a rapid rise of temperatures throughout the month.

APRIL 2017. The tornado season, usually at its peak in the South during April will be subdued this year with generally warm and dry conditions. Water should be utilized in a conservative manner during the growing season, given cooling ocean temperatures and less solar activity. Cool and unsettled weather will persist in New England with snow falling from the Berkshires to the White Mountains. Farther west, the Great Lake states will enjoy mild days though sub-freezing night temperatures will persist. The risk of severe weather is focused on Texas and Oklahoma this month with the chance of several tornado outbreaks. A spring snowstorm is likely for Denver and Minneapolis.

MAY 2017. Beautiful spring weather covers much of the nation this month as sunny days and balmy breezes spread north along the Eastern Seaboard. Coastal onshore winds bring cooler afternoon temperatures there, while sharply warmer temperatures are welcomed farther inland. New England is vulnerable to a brief thunderstorm outbreak that can produce hail and high winds in a few places. In Florida, the storm season begins early this year as easterly trade winds freshen. Most occur along the Sunshine State's Eastern edge by late morning, evolving along the West Coast by late afternoon. Given the Spring onset of such storms, hail and high winds are also possible. Thunderstorms are also focused across the Western Plains in an otherwise dry pattern throughout the nation's heartland. Sunny days and pleasant nights are enjoyed on the West Coast, while dry and hot conditions build in the desert Southwest. Sunny and seasonable temperatures are prevalent across the Great Lake states though folks should be alert to several fast-moving thunderstorm outbreaks during the month.

SUMMER

JUNE 2017. Pacific Ocean temperatures will bring limited rainfall throughout the West and much of the Southern U.S. Drought conditions will gradually return to California's lowlands and the southern Plains. Only Florida and Georgia will receive normal rainfall as tropical trade winds bring daily showers to some places. The Mid-Atlantic, New England and Ohio Valley enjoy sunny and warm weather with cool nights much of the time as the threat of frost has ended. A few days of thunder with the risk of an isolated tornado runs high this year as far west as the Great Lakes where the weather pattern turns hot.

JULY 2017. Much of the nation sizzles in mid-summer heat. Record warmth is felt from New England to the Mid-Atlantic, with only feeble sea breezes cooling communities from Eastport Maine to Ocean City Maryland. Drenching downpours become more numerous from the southern Appalachians to Florida and as far west as New Orleans. Tropical disturbances awaken bringing rain to parts of the desert Southwest but only in mountainous terrain, common with the West's monsoon season. An early start to the hurricane season can also be expected in the Atlantic, with residents along the Gulf Coast and the Florida Panhandle especially vulnerable. Crop yields should be abundant again this year despite hot temperatures, as solar activity is somewhat subdued. The West Coast enjoys strengthening coastal breezes, with pleasant temperatures at the shoreline contrasting blistering heat a few miles inland.

AUGUST 2017. The heat eases somewhat as the Sun's energy wanes with the passing days, lengthening evening shadows. Still, the East experiences near-record heat for a time. Atlantic Ocean water temperatures turn warmer and the risk of a landfalling hurricane is rising again. This is in sharp contrast to ten years of below-normal activity. This probability is preceded by a long spell of wet weather as the east experiences its own monsoonal flow. Above-normal rainfall will be especially apparent at higher elevations away from coastal cities. The weather remains quite dry across the Great Lakes and Plains, with cooler breezes arriving in the northern Rockies by the 20th. Afternoon thunderstorms are common along the continental divide and lightning will trigger some forest fires, which are a part of this natural cycle. Southern California can receive some brief showers from an offshore tropical disturbance.

AUTUMN

SEPTEMBER 2017. Warmer water in the Atlantic Ocean compared to the last ten years brings not only more hurricanes but increases the severity of such storms. The risk of a land-falling hurricane from the Caribbean to New England runs high. At the peak of hurricane season so called "Cape Verde" storms represent some peril, gathering great power crossing the Atlantic. Preceding will be days of soaking rain along the Eastern Seaboard. Farther west, the weather will be much more tranquil with sunny days and crisp nights from the Ohio Valley to the Great Plains. Chilly air advances to the northern Rockies and Great Basin, with a dusting of snow at the highest peaks. California enjoys sunny and pleasant days though brush fires can flare in the South. Monsoonal rains persist at higher elevations in the desert Southwest. Occasional tropical rains fall on south Florida with brisk east winds.

OCTOBER 2017. A gradual end to the hurricane season brings drier weather to the Eastern Seaboard. Warm weather continues there, as balmy southwest winds persist, accompanied by showery spells and occasional thunder. Dry weather is in store for the harvest across the southern plains, though the heat may limit crop production. Better yields occur farther north from Nebraska to the Dakotas. In Idaho and eastern Washington a frost can be expected as colder weather quickens and spreads to the Great Basin. The cold's arrival is associated with an advancing storm crossing the Pacific, bringing snow to the northern Rockies and Cascades. Farther south and away wet weather begins early. Winds are brisk in California, heightening fire danger. Heat persist in Arizona and New Mexico, though evenings turn pleasant.

NOVEMBER 2017. Winter arrives in parts of the West though coastal locations remain balmy. Mountain ranges are covered and a winter storm is possible in Denver which could spawn tornadoes in Texas and Oklahoma. Mild and dry weather is felt east of the Mississippi River and through the lower Ohio Valley. Great temperature contrasts are felt in the Northeast and in particular through New England, where a series of cold fronts pass with chilly rain. The Southeast remains quite warm and dry with seasonal rains decreasing. Afternoon thunderstorms can form near the southwest coast but in general activity diminishes there as well.

WINTER

DECEMBER 2017. Cold and dry weather is expected from Texas to the Great lakes, with light snow likely mid-month in Chicago and Detroit. Cold weather will arrive quietly in New England, though risk of an ice storm is high across the interior. This is less likely along the coast where warmer water temperatures will keep the mercury above freezing. South of the nation's capital, much of the month will be unusually warm and dry, with rising fire danger in Florida. Wet weather will persist along the Gulf Coast. In the West, fine early season skiing is underway in Colorado and Utah, though California's Sierra Nevada receives little snowfall. Fire danger remains high in California with renewed near-drought conditions. The Pacific Northwest is surprisingly dry.

JANUARY 2018. The depth of midwinter cold is felt across the Great Plains and Rocky Mountain states with below zero nights in many places and frigid days. Much of the Great Lakes are partially frozen by the end of the month. Snowfall is light and dry at higher elevations. In the East, the winter pattern contrasts warm and dry weather in the Southeast and a long spell of snowy and cold weather farther north. Snowfall will be above normal from Ohio to New England with double the normal amount in some places, mostly through an ongoing series of light to moderate snow falls. This will likely produce a long-lasting snow cover with little chance for a pronounced thaw. Dry and mild weather can be expected along the West Coast, with the risk for fire remaining high in California.

FEBRUARY 2018. Deep snow and normal temperatures are boons to winter sports enthusiasts in the Northeast. This sharply contrasts unusually warm and dry weather only a short distance away, where pleasant temperatures await travelers escaping winter conditions. In Florida, daily highs easily reach the 70s, with little chance for a frost this year. Brush fires can be a risk on otherwise cloudless days. The worst of the cold is over in the Plains after the 10th. Snow becomes more widespread across the southern and central Rockies as a vortex becomes entrenched in the Great Basin. High pressure remains entrenched along the West Coast as water supplies become strained again. This may foreshadow more serious conditions in the months to come.

The Coefficient of Weirdness
Notes Toward a General Theory of Magic, Part 1

MAGIC IS ONE of the great universals of human life. The earliest records of our past as a species, in Egypt and Mesopotamia and China, are replete with magical rituals, spells and tales of magicians. No anthropologist has ever found any exotic culture that lacks magic. If you try to write magic off as some primitive, superstitious folly, doomed to extinction as science advances, you will write in vain. Magic will outlast you and all your science.

By its very nature, so the philosopher Ludwig Wittgenstein thought, humankind seems to be *a ceremonial animal*, that is, an animal to whom ritual comes as naturally as speaking. Indeed, ritual and speech have many things in common: both make heavy use of symbols, both are highly patterned activities and both are eagerly learned by very young children as tools that extend (or seem to extend) their power over their surroundings.

The other side of the coin is that humankind is also a talking animal. We chatter without ceasing and we have done so in tens of thousands of different languages all over the globe, down through the ages. Children, especially twins and triplets, are even able to create new, private languages of their own, each with its own grammar and vocabulary.

And as with language, so with ritual: children also often create small private rituals of their own, usually out of sight of their parents and other adults.

In these facts—I dare say, in these *biological* facts—lie some of the foundations of any general theory of magic. Among other tasks, such a theory should set forth the principles on which human beings naturally design their rituals and ceremonies, or craft their charms and spells.

This and several more essays spread over subsequent issues of *The Witches' Almanac* will set out several parts of such a theory.

Voces Magicae

Throughout the world, cultures generally distinguish the language used in *numinous* areas of life, for example, in magic or religion, from ordinary, everyday language. Sometimes a magic spell must only be whispered or chanted, never spoken aloud in an ordinary way with an ordinary voice. A religious or magical ritual may even employ a distinct sacred language, like Church Latin in the Roman Catholic Mass (before Vatican II) or Sanskrit in Hindu rituals.

In some cultures, that sacred language is completely different from the everyday spoken language, and thus wholly unintelligible to the people, as for example, Church Latin is to Catholics who speak only Polish or Hungarian. In others, though the sacred language is a dead language, it is closely enough related to the everyday language of the country that a listener can get the general drift of what the sentences mean, as Catholic speakers of Italian or Spanish can from Church Latin. In still other cases the sacred language may merely be a more or less archaic variant of the everyday language of a community, as is the ritual use of the old-fashioned English of the King James Bible by some Protestant ministers. And there are other possibilities as well.

The anthropologist Bronislaw Malinowski examined one such culture in depth during the years he spent among the Austronesian people of the Trobriand Islands, which lie slightly to the east of New Guinea. There he learned the native language, *Kilivila*, and studied the Trobriand way of life. He was fascinated by their very complex system of magic and spent many hours recording spells and rituals, persuading the professional magicians who deployed them to expound to him their meaning and wider significance. Eventually he came up with "an ethnographic theory of the magical word" to account for what he had found there. (See his *Coral Gardens and their Magic*, 1935, especially vol. 2, pp. 211–250.)

Everyday speech in Kilivila was perfectly intelligible to the natives, and eventually also to Malinowski, but the variant of that language used in Trobriand magic was far from clear to most native speakers of Kilivila. It differed from everyday speech through "its richness of phonetic, rhythmic, metaphorical and alliterative effects, with its weird cadences and repetitions." It made heavy use of words that were hard or impossible for even the expert native magician to explain or translate. (Think of magic words in English like *abracadabra* or *hocus pocus* or *rentum tormentum*.) In these spells "obscurity is a virtue and non-grammatical formations impart a peculiar and characteristic flavor and value." The sentences of these spells do

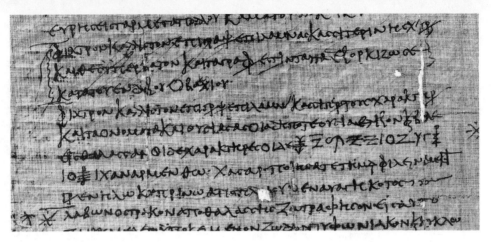

not communicate any specific messages from one person to another, as ordinary speech does, but rather they are used to "inject" the power of magic into ordinary things, setting them apart from a mundane to a magical use.

The Trobriand Islanders held that a spell's magical power was inherent in the words of the spell itself, uttered exactly as the first magicians that ever walked the earth were thought to have uttered them in their ancient, primeval Kilivilan language. When a magician utters such a spell now, its power is carried forth on the breath that he must exhale in order to speak. By physically directing his exhaled words into or onto some external object or person, he applies the power of the spell to that object or person. No such power is conveyed when he uses every day, common Kilivilan speech to talk about everyday matters.

Naturally, a primeval spell of such uncommon power will not be couched in ordinary, common, everyday words. All magical spells of the Trobriand Islanders show "a very considerable *coefficient of weirdness*, strangeness and unusualness." This adds to its power.

By contrast, ordinary mundane speech has a high "coefficient of intelligibility." Both coefficients are at work whenever anyone speaks. The important thing is which coefficient predominates.

Malinowski's happy phrase, coefficient of weirdness, is well worth remembering by any theorist of magic. It is not just in the Trobriand Islands that magical rituals and spells gain power in part from their heightened coefficient of weirdness.

Rhythmic Symbols

But that is not all. Malinowski saw that these spells of the Trobriand Islanders also had an esthetic side to them. Compared to everyday speech, they are uncommonly rich in rhythm, rhyme and alliteration, in the subtle use of metaphor and metonymy. They are paced with cryptic allusions to Trobriand mythology and to the mighty works of the islanders' ancestral magicians. In short, these spells were works of sophisticated verbal art. When a magician carries out a magic ritual, he performs a work of art which has a verbal component, but also components of posture, movement, place, time and other such things. The

Magical Art is a true art in the esthetic sense of the word.

Yet, unlike present-day poetry in English, these magic spells are meant to get things done. They are what philosophers and linguists call *performative* speech acts. We still have a few performative acts of speech in modern American culture—but only a very few, mostly in the realms of law and religion. When two people exchange vows and an authorized agent of the state pronounces them married, the very words have caused a real change, a change that has unyielding consequences in the material world. They are no longer just two people in a relationship: they are now also a married couple, which they were not before that performative act. When a witness in a courtroom swears to tell the truth, the whole truth, and nothing but the truth, he brings about a change in his physical reality: any false testimony of his which would formerly have been a mere lie, is now a act of perjury, a crime with heavy material punishments. In traditional cultures that have no writing, many more kinds of speech acts are performative. Among them are magical rituals and spells.

As in any other art, an esthetic response can be called forth in the viewer or hearer by the highly skillful use of meaningful signs and symbols (including words), and also by the highly skillful use of mere patterns devoid of any meaning. In some traditional cultures, baskets are woven from reeds, and the weaver will weave the reeds into extremely subtle and complex patterns, plainly visible on the outside of the finished basket. This is an art of pure pattern, if (as often happens) the woven patterns themselves have no meaning in the weaver's culture. In other cultures, the basket-weaver's art may produce pictures or symbols of mythological beings, or even represent the flow of a myth's narrative, on the surface of a basket. Here we have an art of form and symbol together. And finally, a storyteller may choose to tell a myth in unadorned words only, without rhyme or rhythm, and yet tell it with such skill that his words alone make a strong esthetic impression on his hearers. Since his words and sentences have meaning, his art is one of pure symbol.

Meaningless patterns and meaningful symbols both have their uses in magic, as in art generally. My examples were from basket-weaving and story-telling, but other examples could have been taken from dance and music and song. Patterns and symbols are universals of human culture. They are also universals of magic.

Looking Forward

This is a good place to end the first of these *Notes Toward a General Theory of Magic*. The next Note should appear in next year's issue of *The Witches' Almanac*. It will examine two of the most useful laws of magic—the Law of Similarity and the Law of Contact, as Sir James George Frazer called them in *The Golden Bough*. To illustrate these two laws we will also take a close look at an actual thousand-year-old Anglo-Saxon ritual, the magic spell usually called *Æcerbot*, or in modern English, "Field-Remedy."

–ROBERT MATHIESEN

Waynaboozhoo

The Great Flood Story of the Ojibwa —
A traditional tale of good and evil

OUT OF THE FOUR elements—fire, earth, air and water—it has been said that water is the strongest because it will eventually overcome the other three. The profound impact of water is garnering new respect during this time of global change, with rising ocean levels and cycles of floods around the planet drawing increased attention—but it is also a source of fear.

Despite the destruction in the aftermath of floods, there is a cleansing quality, a renewal in the end. Floods are a part of many spiritual and historical traditions from all around the world, dating back to the dawn of time. Noah's ark and the *Epic of Gilgamesh* are two well-known examples of the Great Flood leitmotif. The legendary floods can be linked to divine intervention: a deity uses floods to drown evil. The Ojibwa Native Americans, who live in Minnesota and Wisconsin, have their Great Flood story:

In days long past, the world was filled with evil, far worse than in modern times. All men and women lost respect for each other. Gitchie Manito, the Great Creator Spirit, grew sad, then angry. He sent a great flood to purify the world, decreeing the world could be rebuilt only if a clump of the Old Earth could be found. The waters rose and covered all of the evil. The animals were allowed to survive along with just one lone human being, a man named Waynaboozhoo.

For more days than he could count Waynaboozhoo clung to a floating log. He wondered what to do as he gazed around, seeing only water. Finally he dove down and tried to find a handful of Old Earth, so he could begin to build a new world. The water was too deep; he couldn't reach the bottom. Maang, the loon, offered to help. Maang soon resurfaced, announcing in a mournful song that he couldn't find the bottom either. Zhon-gwayzh, the mink, then thought he could help, but he was also unsuccessful. Ni-gig, the otter, and finally Mi-zhee-kay, the turtle, tried but none of the animals could reach the Old Earth beneath the water.

Then Wa-zhushk, the muskrat, the smallest and most timid of all, swam forward and asked if he might help.

The others doubted he could do it, but said he could try anyway. Wa-zhushk disappeared into the deep waters and was gone a very, very long time. At last, Waynaboozhoo saw the tiny Wa-zhushk floating on the surface of the deep water. He grabbed him, amazed and overjoyed to find a clump of mud grasped Wa-zhushk's tiny paw. Then Waynaboozhoo realized the muskrat was dead.

With a mixture of hope and sadness, Waynaboozhoo took the Old Earth from the muskrat's paw and placed it on Mi-zhee-kay's shell. Suddenly four winds blew from all the four corners of the sky. The mud stretched across the turtle's back, growing larger and larger as the waters receded. When the winds became calm, there was a huge and beautiful island in the center of the great water. Gratefully, Waynaboozhoo sang a sacred song of thanksgiving:

Oh Great Spirit,
Whose voice I hear in the winds,
Whose breath gives life to everyone,

Make me ever ready to come
before you,

With clean hands and a straight eye.
Make me wise so that I may
understand,
What lessons you have hidden,
In each leaf and rock.

The animals began to dance around the island and it was soon covered with lush plants and all that was needed to begin a New Earth. Wa-zhushk, who sacrificed his own life to save the others, was elevated forever to a place of great honor among the animals. Waynaboozhoo asked Gitchie Manito, the Creator Spirit, to also honor Mi-zhee-kay for holding the New Earth on his back. Thus Turtle was then blessed with the ability to live comfortably in both worlds: the water and the land.

–COMPILED BY MARINA BRYONY

91

Cemetery Symbols and Funerary Art

Voices for the Dead

SILENT, POTENT and intriguing, symbols have always been deeply significant. Creating and sharing them speaks to a primal deep-seated human need to communicate ideas. The first hunter-gatherers used the earliest symbols in prehistoric times. Over time many thousands of symbols both sacred and secular appeared. Symbols reveal status, authority and purpose and are a part of all societies with a hierarchal structure. The word symbol comes from the Latin and Greek root words symbolus, which means "to mark" and sumballein, meaning "to compare or toss together." The idea is that a symbol suggests something deeper and other than itself.

Over the past several years The Witches' Almanac has included a featured symbol appropriate to the theme of each issue. These carefully selected symbols are gateways to a deeper understanding of the Craft. Mediating on and sharing symbols can benefit those who would follow the paths of magic and adeptship in a variety of ways. This year the selection features a variety of different symbols which might appeal to readers who are taphophiles—those who enjoy cemeteries and appreciate funeral traditions. These symbols are popular in funerary art and have been selected from interesting images on monuments in both historic and contemporary cemeteries.

These symbols are about love and respect. Sometimes they express the last wishes of the deceased in leaving a final message for the living. More often, the funerary symbols express a desire to leave a memory, a record of a life now ended. Funerary symbols express an enduring love, respect and sense of loss for the deceased by the loved ones who remain. Consider reflecting upon graveyard symbols for insight into the meaning of life. The symbols might also be useful in developing mediumship, the ability to communicate with the afterlife. Perhaps a favorite funerary symbol can be adopted as a source of inspiration for making the best use of our most precious and transient asset—time.

Popular symbols in Funerary Art

Anchor—marks the way to a secret meeting place.

Angels—guardians of the dead, spiritual comfort.

Arch—victory of life.

Arrow—reminder of mortality and vulnerability.

Bee—from Greek mythology, the bee is the soul itself and provides a bridge from the world of nature to the afterlife.

Bridge—a very old symbol, the link between Earth and Heaven.

Butterfly—a short life in three stages, the caterpillar, chrysalis and finally the winged butterfly.

Candle—eternal light of life.

Cardinal—a passion for life.

Chain—truth.

Chariot—a journey taken by the soul.

Circle—never ending existence.

Clouds—conceals the mystery of the afterlife.

Comedy and Tragedy Masks—memory of a performer.

Cross—ties to a variety of spiritual beliefs both Pagan and Christian with messages of faith, love and choices.

Deer—regeneration, happiness, guidance through the darkness.

Dogs—loyalty and service. Dogs have been popular in funerary art since medieval times.

Dove—a common motif, usually portrayed descending to represent the Holy Spirit.

Dolphin—connects to the concept of resurrection.

Dragon—triumph over sin and evil.

Draperies and Curtains—lingering of mourning, grief is inconsolable.

Eagle—courage and perhaps an affinity with the military.

Fallen Leaves—sadness, melancholy.

Fish—faith.

Flower—beauty and frailty of life.

Frog—reveling in the senses and worldly pleasures.

Hammer—power of creation, a builder.

Hands—a last farewell.

Heart—love, mortality, courage, connection to God.

Hooped Snake (Ouroboros)—eternity.

Horse—travel, generosity, valor.

Hourglass—time has stopped for the deceased; mortality.

Keys—provide the means to enter heaven.

Lamb—usually reserved for children, symbolizes gentleness and innocence.

Lighthouse—someone who inspired and guided others.

Lion—divine power, a guardian of the soul.

Olive Branch—peace.

Open Book—an embodiment of faith.

Owl—wisdom, a long life.

Peacock—incorruptibility.

Pineapple—hospitality, the deceased was a good host.

Pyramid—eternity.

Rooster—awakening, a resurrection.

Squirrel, usually holding an acorn—striving for spiritual progress.

Shamrock or Clover—the deceased was Irish or had luck as a gambler.

Shell—a symbol of pilgrimage, protection.

Ship—resting place of a sailor.

Skull—final death, facing sin, mortality.

Steps—climbing and ascending to a higher level, a better place.

Sun—the beginning and ending of life, sunrise, sunset.

Wheat—timely harvest.

−Esther Neumeier

More information on cemetery symbols can be found on our website at http://The WitchesAlmanac.com/AlmanacExtras/.

94

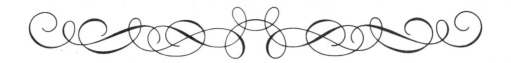

The Margate Grotto
A Mystery Spelled In Shells

UNDERGROUND WORLDS are a recurrent and timeless theme which can be traced through the cosmography of nearly every culture around the globe. The thought of mysterious sunless regions accessed only through hidden openings so fascinated the gentry in Europe during the eighteenth century that building underground grottos became something of a fad. Called "follies" to reflect their purpose as amusing frivolities, these basement-like structures were often decorated with shells and stones.

They were always located on the grounds of wealthy estates.

In 1835 a farm worker in Margate, Kent in South East England was laboring in an isolated field. It was open land and had never been the site of a great house or castle according to the historical records of the area. He was baffled when his spade suddenly broke through into hollow ground. There seemed to be something opening beneath the surface, yet he could see nothing unusual.

News of this odd situation quickly

spread through the small seaside village. The local school master arrived to see what all of the fuss was about, accompanied by his young son. Seeing that there was indeed something to the worker's story, it was agreed that the boy would be lowered into the hole, which had been enlarged by then to reveal a cavern. Carrying a candle young Joshua shouted he could see rooms and rooms all covered in hundreds of thousands of shells. The adults went down to inspect the situation for themselves and made a stunning discovery. There were elaborate mosaics of stars, spirals, the Sun, flowers and geometric shapes. Oyster shells, limpets, whelks, mussels, scallops and cockles which could have been collected from the local beaches, were meticulously arranged with winkle shells, which would have had to have been brought in from other areas, to be combined into the beautiful works of art. Altars, vaulted ceiling, a rotunda and passages connecting multiple rooms revealed at least 2000 square feet of wall space incredibly covered in innumerable shells. A tremendous amount of time, effort and resources had been dedicated to creating the long hidden underground grotto.

The schoolmaster was very forward thinking. He immediately seized the opportunity and acted quickly to purchase the farm land. He had a hunch that there could be financial success through promoting it as a successful tourist attraction. Margate is located just North of Folkston, which even then was already a popular seaside resort. By 1837 the former teacher had opened and renovated the grotto, creating an easily accessible walk-in entrance where he could charge admission. His idea proved to be a brilliant one. The Margate Shell Grotto is still operating and draws many tourists today. Open regularly the attraction now includes a café, gift shop and museum.

The mystery endures though. No one has ever been able to determine for sure who built the Margate Grotto or why. Some scientists and archeologists claim it dates back 3000 years. Others say it shows a connection with a Mexican culture. It has even been speculated that the grotto is up to twelve thousand years old. Others relate it to Pagan religious rites, The Knights Templar, astrological calendars or even the private retreat created by the visions of a rich madman. During the 1930s Spiritualists held séances here, but there doesn't seem to be a record of their findings.

In recent years, water damage has dulled the color and luster of the shells in some places. They are still amazing and beautiful though, and conservation work is underway to restore them. Preservation efforts have so far taken precedence over suggestions that radiocarbon dating could accurately determine the age of the shells. Presently it is thought this would be too expensive. So instead visitors can continue, as they have for 180 years, to give their imaginations and intuition free reign as they wander through the long-hidden underground building at Margate. Was it a hideout decorated by pirates? Were the shells encoded messages for smugglers showing where buried treasure might be found? Or do the shells invoke supernatural forces? What do you think?

–GRANIA LING

Spirits and Ghosts

Fervor and Infatuation in Contemporary Norway

ON SUNDAYS in Norway nowadays the churches are nearly empty. Although most modern Norwegians will identify themselves as Evangelical Lutherans, the country has gradually grown very secular and agnostic during the 21st century. Belief in the Christian God, statistics reveal, has declined. Norway's Humanist Association, an atheist group, even recently ran a national campaign relating God to trolls and Santa Claus as a way to promote the idea that religion is superstition and about to die out completely, as Karl Marx and Sigmund Freud predicted it would.

Not so. Instead, faith and the need to experience and express religious feelings and spirituality have taken an entirely different track. Ghosts and spirits are filling the void. Paranormal phenomena are increasing throughout Norway. A steadily growing number of people are seeking advice about an acceleration of mystical happenings which defy physical laws. Forces that can't be seen or understood impact daily life, many Norwegians claim. Although ghosts have been around for centuries the focus on them is going through a resurgence throughout this Scandinavian country.

A group of teenage science students travel around one especially haunted region near the town of Moss tracing ghosts with electronic meters and regularly posting videos of their discoveries on the Internet. Recently, staff members at a tourist agency in Moss described weird happenings such as strange odors, inexplicable noises and the movement of objects, especially travel brochures. The workers noted the German brochures were always inexplicably shifted to the front of the display, although there were few German speaking visitors. Plumbers and electricians checked out the building and found nothing amiss. The situation became so strange that the employees grew fearful. A clairvoyant was consulted. She determined the source of the trouble was the spirit of a German soldier who had been lingering on the premises since working there during World War II. After the building was spiritually cleansed, the activity ceased and peace was restored.

Perhaps an ingrained thirst, the primal longing for spiritual support, is leading to this resurgence of Pagan pre-Christian beliefs around the country. The Lutheran Church has recently developed a liturgy of ghosts to help parishioners cleanse their homes of unwanted spiritual presences. Norway's Royal Family has even become involved. One princess has begun to assist people in reaching out to the spirit world.

A television program, *The Power of Spirits*, airs each Sunday and draws at least a half million viewers, a huge percentage of the country's total population of five million. The show's host, Tom Stromnaess, says "All of this is for real concerning forces that can't be seen or understood." Mr. Stromnaess tells of visiting many sites where paranormal energies are actively at work. He speaks of hundreds of viewers who contact him for help in dealing with haunted homes or workplaces and says that "All of these people can't be crazy." There is a great demand for the services of professional mediums who can earn 800 Norwegian Kroner, about $98 per hour, for ghost cleansing and spirit communication.

The courts in Norway became involved recently when a homebuyer in the town of Vinstra complained that he was duped into buying a haunted house and should have been notified about the annoying ghosts. The judge was unmoved though, ruling against the alleged mystical events being a defect in the property. The plaintiff did not receive a refund.

Interest in ghosts and the occult is so strong that in November 2015 Oslo hosted its first "Alternative Expo," including hundreds of practitioners of alternative faiths and various metaphysical topics. Perhaps it is because of the starkness of Norway's long, dark winters which necessitate a focus on the practicalities of survival, but most of the spirit visitors don't seem particularly benevolent. At best they resemble playful but spiteful poltergeists, at worst they appear rather sinister.

—CATIE SALTMARSH

Revealing the Secret Mysteries

THE MYSTERIOUS concept of Da'at in the Qabalah attracts thrill seekers and scholars alike. At times teachers will deliberately avoid speaking on the topic, leaving students all the more eager to obtain its secret mysteries. This piece sets out to reveal.

The first secret mystery to reveal is that there are no secrets, only mysteries. Simple awareness is the secret to stepping onto the path of Mysticism. Once on the path, each of us is our own teacher and our own guide.

The second secret mystery is that we choose all of what we experience. Knowledge of Da'at is the attainment of the perspective of Da'at. The Knowledge attained through the perspective of Da'at is that perspective dictates reality. Perspective and hence reality itself, is personal. Any suggestion of a shared reality results from an agreed upon perspective between individuals, groups, cultures. Often this is completely subconscious, shared concepts learned and taught through the ages, the self-woven fabric of human nature. But the Da'at

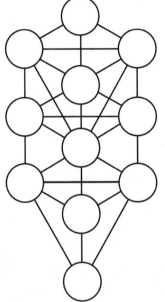

perspective of Creation reveals to us that we are not at all constrained by these preconceptions. We are all endowed with the power of reality-dictating choice.

The third secret mystery is that freewill and fate are both true. Freewill is our choice of perspective. Fate is the myriad of possibilities presented to us, infinite perspectives of a whole we can only comprehend piecemeal. Everything we can conceive of is within the realm of possibility. Fate is the totality of possibilities. We navigate fate with our free will, which results in a progression of soul experiences. Free will dictates the near-term; fate dictates the long-term.

The fourth secret mystery is that the illusion of reality is real. The perspective looking from below to above is that of the fallen tree, the Tree of Knowledge of Good and Evil. Kingdom/Malkut sits apart from the Heavens and Knowledge/Da'at is absent. But Knowledge/Da'at isn't non-existent, rather it is unmanifest from this perspective. The perspective looking from above to below reveals the perfected tree, the Tree of Life; Knowledge/Da'at is present and Kingdom/Malkut is absent. But Kingdom/Malkut isn't non-existent, it is un-manifest from this perspective. Both perspectives are real and as inseparable from each other as a person and their shadow.

Our higher selves agree to suspend our disbelief and accept that we are distinct from the Creator in order to experience Creation. As our soul experiences accumulate they build and ascend. Eventually perspectives of the higher worlds disclose the Oneness of Creation and we come full circle, the mystery revealed.

–Izun

YHVH is One. YHVH is All. We are all YHVH. We are all One.
Treat yourself and others accordingly.

The Fathomless Mystery of the Sea

WHEREVER WE LIVE, the sea is our spiritual home. Whether we think in terms of the ethereal elements of the water margin or the dark depths of the ocean bed, the sea makes us constantly aware of the fathomless mystery of this strange marine world.

Nowhere else was this image brought home to us than with the events surrounding missing aircraft MH370 that focussed the world's attention on the Indian Ocean. Although the youngest of the major oceans, it is the third largest covering approximately 20 percent of the water on the Earth's surface and contains some of the deepest ocean trenches on the planet. Its deepest points being the Diamantina Trench at 26,401 feet deep and the Sunda Trench at 23,812–25,344 feet. In this deep, dark place the passengers of that aircraft still lie entombed in their watery grave, known to seafarers as Davy Jones's Locker.

These are awe-inspiring statistics but how can we put this sort of information into a *magical* perspective? Here we move away from the water's edge and confront the power of the deep by means of pathworking, but one of the first exercises we must carry out is the creation of a protective charm using the image of the sea crab.

Le crabe enragé protection charm:

This is one of the most common sea-creatures seen on the beaches and can be found in the highest rock pools to depths of 200 feet in the sea. In summer they move out into the brackish waters of estuaries and salt marshes, remaining higher up the shore and on mudflats when the tide drops, where they survive in small pools or burrows. These little creatures are survivalists that can re-grow lost limbs and are both scavengers and ingenious predators. In Greek mythology, the crab was sent to distract

Hercules when he was fighting the Hydra. The hero's foot crushed the crab, but as a reward for its efforts Hera placed it among the stars. The zodiacal symbol of Cancer represents the crab's claws.

From a magical perspective, the Sun's entry into Cancer marks the Summer Solstice, the longest day in the northern hemisphere (in the southern hemisphere it marks the Winter Solstice and the shortest day). Shore crabs are most active at night and high tide and are, not surprisingly, ruled by the Moon. The French name is *le crabe enrage* and it is from the animal's habit of waving its open pincers threateningly when disturbed that we take the image necessary for our magical rite of protection.

At the highest level of the tide take a small, airtight jar and fill it with seawater. If you live inland, national newspapers give information about the tides and a brine solution can be made from sea salt. This is your 'holy' water and its power is drawn directly from the sea, so there is no need for cleansing or charging.

Now take an image of a crab, the zodiacal symbol for Cancer or a picture of *le crabe enragé*. If you take this from a book, magazine or newspaper, make a photocopy to prevent anything appearing on the reverse side of the image. If you prefer, a small piece of jewellery can be used and once charged, will afford you the protection of the crab to carry around on your person.

If the spell is for the general protection of your home, place the image of the crab into the sea-water and screw the jar tightly to prevent seepage. The crab represents it/you defending your quarter and although small, *can* pack a wallop with those pincers! Prepare the spell by moonlight and as the image absorbs the water, visualise the crab coming alive to challenge any enemies or intruders—on both the physical and psychic levels. If the ink runs and distorts the picture, don't worry, it merely means the essence of the crab itself is entering the water.

Allow the salt water to stand on a window sill where it can catch both sun and moonlight for seven high tides before using it to sprinkle over all the entry points to your home including the chimney. Use whatever chant or intonation you feel comfortable with in order to 'fix' the spell to protect against whatever you feel is a threat, or use the words:

I [Magical Name] cast this barrier of protection around myself, my loved

ones, and my home, across which no hostile or malevolent forces dare cross.

If you are charging a pendent to wear on a chain or key-ring, then the image should remain in the seawater for the same amount of time but adapt the 'fix' accordingly. Remember that salt water is corrosive and do not use anything that could be damaged, since this would lessen the potency of the spell.

Abyssal Mysteries

From beach-combing to the exploration of underwater hot springs known as hydrothermal vents, we interact with the sea at a level that provides its own magical comfort-zone. In 1977 however, scientists made a stunning discovery on the bottom of the Pacific Ocean – vents pouring hot, mineral rich fluids from beneath the sea floor. These vents were discovered to be inhabited by previously unknown organisms thriving in the absence of sunlight, forever changing our understanding of life on Earth. Because

these vents act as a natural plumbing system that transports heat and chemicals from the interior of the Earth, they help regulate global ocean chemistry.

This aspect of the Deep can perhaps be compared with what is often described as the reverse Tree of Life, accessed only by descending into the Abyss, but it can also be used as a path-working we can experience from the comfort of an armchair. Using an armchair represents the close confines of a submersible, while the green or blue 'stand-by' light on an electrical appliance in a darkened room simulates the glow from the cockpit. We need no other magical 'props' other than our imagination as we visualise ourselves descending down into this fabulous Otherworld.

Reviewer Andy Lloyd shrewdly observed: "What strikes me is the amount of science running through [the book]. To understand nature is to live as a part of nature, and ultimately to become one with its changing patterns and cycles, to synchronise one's own psychic or magical energy with natural tidal forces and the elements. The world of the sea-witch is not confined to the shore and the water margin. It is a multi-dimensional world of light and shadow, of reality and illusion, where we have moved into the subjective world of the spirit – a rich fishing ground for those who trawl in these inner seas. The Mystery is now within and around us" ... The learning is multi-disciplinary, and feels almost as if one were studying a textbook written by a poet. Yet the science collated in these pages is interesting and pragmatic."

The sea *is* a dark and dangerous environment but it is also a very magical place. Its energies can be used to sooth emotions, open up spiritual and psychic portals and be a force that can be harnessed to bring about change. This unknown and untamed element of our planet is possibly the most magical element of all but it constantly draws us into its heart. "I must go down to the sea again ..."

–MELUSINE DRACO

105

Bloody Mary

The Ghost of Maison Dieu House

IN A TOWN as old as Dover, in a county as venerable as Kent, that the spectres of the past rub shoulders with the present is, if not exactly taken for granted, at least commonly accepted. Today Maison Dieu House sits serenely in Jacobean splendour beneath the grandeur of Dover Castle but its peaceful exterior belies the notion that it was once the site of a brutal murder; a murder that still lingers in the bright and peaceful civic building of today in the form of ghostly footsteps pacing an empty chamber, paintings flying off the walls and a ringing doorbell with no one at the door.

For the officers at the Town Council now housed in the building, these almost daily brushes with the past are so much a part of their working lives that uncanny happenings go almost unnoticed. The bell rings of its own accord to the distinctive tune of Westminster Chimes at least several times a week and the near daily sound of frantic pacing coming from an empty council chamber is no longer remarked upon. A paranormal investigation in 2007 revealed the presence of no fewer than five spirits but the most striking of these seems to be that of the young Nanny, Mary Grey, who met her doom here during the Glorious or Bloodless Revolution of William of Orange—an event which sadly proved to be neither for Bloody Mary, the Ghost of

Maison Dieu House. This is her story.

The Legend takes us back to 1688, a time when tensions were high in Dover and the streets were alive with secrets and plots. By the autumn rumours and whispers spoke of the imminent arrival of a new king. Soon it was clear William of Orange would leave Holland to take the throne from his uncle and father in law, King James. In answer, King James' Privy Council hatched a counterplot to prevent this and in their line of fire was Thomas Papillion. Maison Dieu House had been built by the Royal Navy in 1665 to house the Agent Victualler and this year Thomas Papillion was serving in this capacity.

A prominent merchant and campaigner for civil and religious freedoms as M.P. for Dover and then for London, by all accounts Thomas Papillion was an upright and principled man. Jane Papillion was a kind and loving mother and a good wife to Thomas. If she had any faults, they lay in her disinterest in the politics and public affairs that were the mainstay of her husband's existence. She was fond, however, of entertaining and it was in her role as hostess that she came into her own. October 1688 saw her very much looking forward to the start of the social season but this was to be short lived.

Many people came to Maison Dieu House to see Thomas during this time of political unrest but one recent figure had come to concern Jane. For some time, Thomas had been receiving a green-cloaked visitor late at night at the back door. One moonlit evening, as the cloak blew in the autumn wind, Jane caught a glimpse of the beautiful woman hidden beneath. Shortly after, when Thomas asked Jane to take the children to stay at the family seat ten miles away, she flatly refused to go. Not only was the social season just getting under way, she could not help believing that her husband was plotting to replace her with the beautiful green-cloaked woman.

Rejected and desperate, Jane confided her fears to Mary Grey, the children's Nanny. Wanting to reassure her mistress, Mary vowed to discover all she could about these secret liaisons. Late one night she crept into Thomas's study, hiding herself in a cupboard. Her wait was short and Thomas soon returned, pouring himself a large whiskey. Moments later Mary could hear a rap at the window. She peered through the crack in the cupboard. Sure enough, it was the beautiful cloaked stranger. Mary always had the utmost respect for her master but was on the verge of heartbreak herself until she heard the woman utter the words, "William of Orange has set sail for Dover." Then she heard Thomas confirm that William would be staying at Maison Dieu House as previously agreed before taking the throne in London. With this information, the beautiful woman drew her cloak and disappeared back into the night. At once Mary understood that Thomas had asked his wife Jane to leave the house with their children out of fear for their safety. As soon as Thomas retired for the night, Mary crept back to her room. The next day, Mary told Jane all she had learned the

night before. Jane was delighted and after embracing Mary with unusual gratitude she instructed the staff to prepare to leave for the country the next morning.

When morning came they all set out. Jane and the younger children were in the front carriage and Mary Gray was in the rear with the older son. Just as they reached the harbour he begged Mary to get the driver to return to Maison Dieu House for some Latin translations he had been working on. Mary could refuse the children nothing and once inside she dashed to the attic rooms to retrieve the books and papers. As Mary glanced out of the window overlooking the rear gardens she saw the beautiful green-cloaked woman being arrested by soldiers from the castle. From the attic, she could see still more soldiers hiding all around the grounds behind the house. Mary ran back to the carriage and told the driver to carry on with her charge without her. She would have to stay and warn Thomas.

Mary paced the upper floors frantically as she waited for her master to return. Darkness was falling when she bravely and silently returned to her hiding place in the study cupboard. When Thomas eventually returned Mary could hear he was not alone but in the company of the former Mayor. Spying more soldiers entering the back garden, Mary sprang from her hiding place next to the back door just as it was forced open. The sound of musket fire rang out and Mary's blood-soaked body fell to the ground in front of her master. She had saved his life by absorbing the shot meant for him.

William of Orange never did reach Dover that night. Bad weather forced his ship to carry on past Dover to Devon. He landed in Torbay on the 5th of November, 1688 and was crowned King of England on April 11, 1689.

The family of Thomas and Jane prospered but sightings of Mary Grey's ghost began almost before she was buried. Over time, however, the story became tied up with that told by R. H. Barham, the author of "The Ingoldsby Legend." The Lay of the Old Woman Clothed in Grey is set in Dover and mentions Maison Dieu House. In it, Barham relates how the spectre of an old woman in grey sits astride a barrel of wine with a bag of gold held in her right hand, which she proffers politely to all who happen to see her. While the grey lady of the Ingoldsby tale might seem a more colourful character at first glance, the real Mary Grey, Doer's Bloody Mary, has a good deal more substance. To those who are privy to her ways, she is as much a part of Maison Dieu House today as the very floorboards upon which she still paces.

–SARAH SIMPSON-ENOCK

देवी

Devi the supreme being in the Shakta tradition of Hinduism
I (Devi) have created all worlds at my will, without being urged by any
higher being, and I dwell within them.
I permeate the earth and heaven, all created entities with my greatness, and
dwell in them as eternal and infinite consciousness.
—DEVI SUKTA, RIGVEDA 10.125.8

TRUE THOMAS THE RHYMER

Prophet of Legend

THE REMARKABLE STORY of Thomas the Rhymer and his gift of prophecy has been told and retold since the thirteenth century. It originates in a part of the world steeped in history and magic. Three mountain peaks called the Eildon Hills overlook a valley near the River Tweed in the Lowlands of Scotland. Rising 1300 feet, the Hills are visible from many miles away. They are named for the very old Roman military base of Trimontium. Once the Romans were vanquished many legends centered around this strangely beautiful area. One of the most popular, enduring and endearing, involves Thomas Lermont who lived from about 1220–1298, near the village of Earlston on the North side of the triple hills.

It all began when he was resting on a grassy slope one warm afternoon. As he dozed, the Queen of Elfland, clad in green, approached him. He arose and bowed to her. She invited Thomas to visit a magical cavern where he encountered many wonders and terrors, including wading through dark lakes of blood to arrive at a magnificent and bright castle. After what seemed to be a mere day or two, the Elven Queen guided Thomas back to the road home, blessing him with a gift of prophecy and a tongue that would never lie. Thomas discovered that he had been away for seven years. He explained where he had been and was astounded to find that everyone believed him.

The intriguing part of this account is that Thomas began to accurately foretell the future. He often delivered his predictions in the form of whimsical rhymes and riddles, hence earning him the title of Thomas the Rhymer. True Thomas was added to his label because his numerous prophecies have come to pass throughout the centuries. Thomas' prophetic poetry began as an oral tradition, but eventually was collected and preserved along with those of other well-known seers.

On March 16, 1285 Thomas made an incredible prediction while visiting Dunbar Castle. His hosts asked him to describe the next day. In a trance

True thomas he pulld aff his cap,

and Louted low down to his knee:

all hail, thou mighty queen of heaven!

for thy peer on earth i never did see.

he intoned that at noon a blast would come, a calamity heard throughout Scotland bringing the fall of the lofty. Everyone thought this referred to stormy weather. The next morning was mild and clear. Naysayers complained that the 60-something year old prophet had at last struck out for the first time that anyone could remember. However just at noon a messenger arrived with dreadful news. Good King Alexander III, whose reign marked a golden age of peace, had fallen from his horse. Seriously injured, the beloved King died three days later. A time of great suffering and tragedy throughout the land followed Alexander's passing.

Prophecies left by Thomas foretold of the United Kingdom, joining Scotland and England. This took place hundreds of years after his death. He also told of Queen Victoria's meeting with a famous descendant of the Chief of Mar at Stirling Castle in the 19th century to deliver a "kiss of peace." Another prediction regarding an event in 1745 which Thomas said he was happy he would not live to see described the bloody battle of Culloden. He also foretold the joining of the Lochs (Lakes) through the Caledonian Canal which occurred in the 19th century. Once True Thomas pointed to a field far inland and said a ship would dock there, a prophecy which no one could understand. However during the 1930s a dirigible or air ship did land in that very spot.

Looking to the famous Rhymer's prophecies, we still await and wonder about the city of Aberdeen which he said would be washed with a black rain. Some feel this might mean the oil fields in the North Sea bringing their black liquid to boost the faltering economy in the north of Scotland. Others warn that it sounds more like nuclear war or air pollution. The dark cloud of volcanic ash from Iceland which covered the United Kingdom in April 2010 might also have been

what Thomas saw. He also said that "Rome was, London is and Edinburgh shall be." Here True Thomas seems to hint the Scottish capital will one day overshadow London. In 2014 there was a vote in Scotland to become independent and break away from the United Kingdom. This would have made Edinburgh the seat of government. The vote failed by a narrow margin, but strong sentiment is still brewing among separatists.

Two charters dated 1260-80 and 1294 mention Thomas referencing "Thomas de Ercildounson" and "Son and Heir of Thome Rymour of Ercildoun," so there is evidence he was a real person. True Thomas' poetic prophecies hold high esteem in the hearts and words of his countrymen. Over the centuries his popularity and credibility as a soothsayer has rivaled that of Mother Shipton, Nostradamus and even the great Merlin.

–KOO TEMPLETON

Messages In Bamboo
Spiritual Truths and Practical Life Guidance

BAMBOO, the largest member of the Poaceae or grass family, is the source of both elite and humble myths regarding inspiration for discovering the perfect life. It has been said the gods themselves prefer to be visualized through a curtain of bamboo. Even they respect its resilience, strength and flexibility. Through the ages bamboo has earned a place as the ultimate symbol of longevity and good fortune. In the Taoist faith bamboo's survival during storms and other challenging weather is used to illustrate the perfect life. This evergreen plant bends to all of the forces around it, then springs back easily into place. Steadfastness and patience, the most important qualities to be cultivated in order to acquire blessings, have been compared to bamboo. In the sacred art of Chinese calligraphy the bamboo is the first of the four gentlemen (the others are the orchid, plum blossom and chrysanthemum). These four plants, said to embody the perfect qualities of a gentleman, honor the four seasons but are also models for ideal behavior. Bamboo is praised in Chinese art and poetry for its uprightness, tenacity, elegance and simplicity. The hollow interior of the bamboo is likened to an open heart. The Vietnamese have a proverb about bamboo, "When the bamboo is old, the new shoots appear." This is a reminder that Vietnam will never die. A new generation will always follow the annihilation of the old.

For Buddhists who advocate harmlessness and a vegetarian diet, bamboo is on the menu. The tender plant shoots are cooked with rice, often inside the hollow stem of a large bamboo, to create a nutritious staple dish. Bamboo is the primary food source for the beloved panda bear and other animals too. Throughout the Orient those with large enough yards have always added bamboo gardens. It's not merely a plant but an integral part of people's lives. A bamboo forest is thought to offer protection from evil when planted around Shinto Temples in Japan. In Assam, India fermented bamboo paste is a respected folk medicine. In the Philippines and Malaysia bamboo is central to creation myths. The first man and woman are thought to have emerged from a bamboo trunk as it split open.

Writing implements, paper, knitting needles, musical instruments such as flutes and wind chimes, tea whisks, tableware, building construction materials, furniture and fabric are fashioned from the versatile bamboo. The role of bamboo applies to both the mystical and mundane in society. Its message and magic is deep and profound.

Asian philosophy offers Ten Lessons for a Successful Life to be learned from the bamboo. The wise might heed them while facing the complexities and challenges of modern life.

1. What looks small and weak is strong. Bamboo looks diminutive alongside larger trees, but it will endure harsh winters. Often it's the only plant left standing after a storm. Size is not essential for success. Instead, kindness, compassion, light, transparency and cooperation are what matters.

2. Have strong roots, yet be flexible. Bamboo's complex, extensive root structure makes the grove stable.

3. Bend, but don't break. Swaying with the breeze, going with the flow, the bamboo is humble and doesn't struggle against what is. Soon the wind tires while the bamboo remains standing tall.

4. Slow down. Calm the mind amid a busy, demanding environment.

5. Be always ready, present and available.

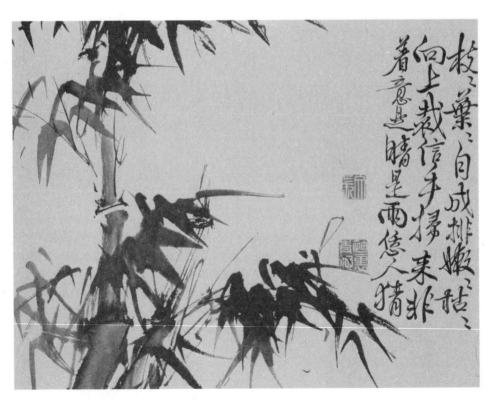

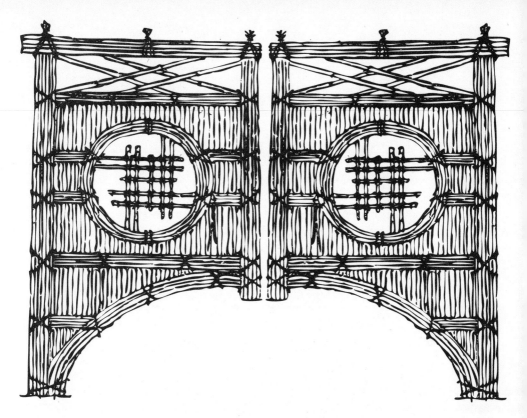

6. There is wisdom in emptiness. The hollow center of the bamboo is a reminder to remain receptive to new growth and different perceptions. Don't be filled with prejudices and old baggage.

7. Smile, life is to be enjoyed. Take time to play. The Japanese character for smiles and laughter contains two small bamboo symbols. Bamboo leaves seem to laugh while rustling in the wind. Bamboo is used to make kites, dolls and other handicrafts which bring pleasure and delight.

8. Commit to growth and renewal, just as the plant expands and continues to grow outward and upward.

9. Express through simplicity.

10. Unleash the power to spring back. In art, the recurrent theme of snow-covered bamboo is important. It's a reminder that after a heavy burden is endured a new season shall arrive. Change is certain.

–LESLIE FORD

The Singing Tower and Spook Hill

A Sacred Journey through Old Florida

"MAKE YOU THE WORLD a bit better or more beautiful because you have lived in it," were the parting words of a beloved grandmother to young Edward William Bok when he left his home in The Netherlands in the mid 19th century to emigrate to America. The grandmother's wise words still echo across time and space. Embossed in the stone archway leading to Bok Tower Gardens in Lake Wales, Florida they greet thousands of visitors each year.

The young immigrant learned English and became the successful and influential editor of *The Ladies' Home Journal*, a position he held for thirty years. By the time he retired in 1919, Bok was fabulously wealthy and wanted to give something back to the adopted country which had been so good to him. Long before Walt Disney flew over Central Florida and envisioned Disney World just 40 miles or so to the North, Edward William Bok recognized the inherent magic and beauty of the area. He purchased 50 acres of land near Lake Wales centered around a hill rising 324 feet above sea level. The hill is the highest point both in Florida and within 60 miles of the Atlantic Ocean between Washington, DC and the Rio Grande River in Texas. The unique energy about the place transcends the spectacular view. Even the birds, squirrels, bobcats, snakes and other wildlife seem oddly tame, calm and enchanted. Perhaps it is

116

due to the underground crystals which are thought to form the hill. Maybe the incomparable tropical gardens, a designated wildlife sanctuary designed by the famed landscape architect Frederick Law Olmstead, work their own elven garden magic.

Atop the hill soars the Gothic style Bok Tower itself. Seven stories high and visible from many miles away it bears an uncanny resemblance to Glastonbury Tor in England. The Singing Tower as it's called is the focal point of the Garden. It houses a glorious carillon with sixty bells and splendid live concerts are enjoyed by visitors daily. The Tower is surrounded by an old world style moat stocked with goldfish. A long reflecting pool magnifies the beauty of the building itself. An unusual reclining sundial surrounded by the signs of the zodiac is etched into the South side, while elaborate carvings of animals, birds and mythological figures add stunning details to the other sides. The only entrance is a brass door embossed with spiritual symbols.

Dedicated for "visitation by the American people" by President Calvin Coolidge at a celebrity-studded gathering on February 1, 1929, Bok Tower and the surrounding gardens have amazed and delighted tourists from all over the world ever since. There is a small admission fee and it offers an intriguing and memorable side trip while visiting the various attractions in Central Florida, especially for metaphysically oriented tourists.

Allow enough time to stop by Spook Hill while driving through the picturesque town of Lake Wales on the way to Bok Tower. Spook Hill has long been promoted as a gravity defying experience. It's free, amusing and can be enjoyed without leaving one's vehicle. A sign explains how to park the car on a white line painted on the road and actually feel it rolling up hill. On a busy day several cars in a row will usually be waiting in line to marvel at this unexplained mystery. Legend tells that the spirits of an Indian Chief and a gigantic alligator are the spooks. It is said they battled to the death because the creature was terrorizing the Chief's village.

–GRANIA LING

Tom Smith's Bon Bons

A Tale of English Magic

A SINGLE JOYOUS experience, an event or encounter which stimulates and uplifts the heart, mind and spirit can sometimes open a kind of magical portal. Usually this happens in a flash. With the mystique and brilliance of a lightning strike those fortunate enough to be blessed in this way experience an immediate and profound change in perception. Their lives might be completely redirected. Occasionally the recipient of such an "aha!" moment will come up with an idea or invention which evolves in a way which uplifts the rest of humanity forever. A little understood and curious fact is that this magical serendipity frequently involves English travelers and adventurers. Perhaps this is because England has for generations been a nation of eccentrics, free thinkers, magicians and scholars attracted to experimenting with all kinds of imaginative studies.

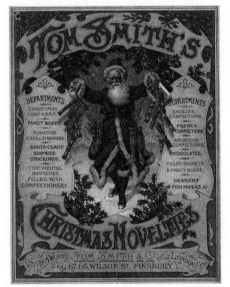

While visiting Paris in 1840, such an English adventurer named Tom Smith, encountered a dining experience which inspired him to create a party favor which has become an essential part of holiday meals in his homeland ever since. Tom was delighted by sugar coated almonds, twisted and wrapped in beautiful tissue. The French called them bon bons and offered them to signal the end of a meal along with dessert. Impressed, Tom took the idea home to Clerkenwell in East London and began a business. He wrapped sugar coated almonds in pretty papers and added hand written love mottos to the tiny packages. Tom's original sayings have been lost in time, but they had mass appeal. In addressing the inner longings of the heart and spirit he might have written:

"Love, madam or sir, like wine will make you drunk if you don't take care."

or perhaps *"No place on the common Earth with ordinary water and air will do where you with true love will fare."*

The product became enormously popular. Sales soared near Christmas. One cold winter's night Tom tossed a log on the hearth fire and listened to the appealing crackle and pop sound it made. This gave him another idea. Adding a bit of drama, a pop as the treats were unwrapped would be

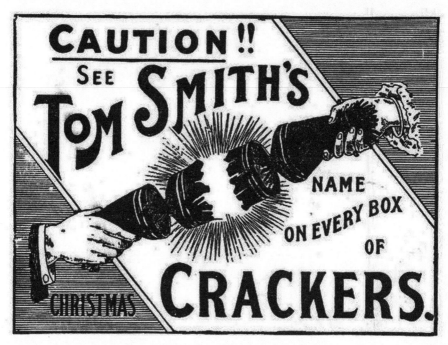

interesting. He experimented until he came up with a simple mechanism that became the signature snap of his bon bons. He renamed them crackers. His original invention has remained the same as crackers, offered as party and holiday favors, are pulled open to this day.

Tom Smith was able to move his family to a more upscale London location in Finsbury Square as the demand for crackers increased. His sons Tom Jr., Walter and Henry eventually inherited and expanded the business. Walter erected a drinking fountain in Finsbury in memory of his mother and father, Mr. and Mrs. Tom Smith. Walter had his father's creative and adventurous spirit. He began to include paper crowns in the crackers. Walter traveled the world in search of new ideas for different candies and unique gifts to add.

As the years passed the Company honored and embraced the changing times. Crackers were created to commemorate the suffragettes, heroic figures linked to the victory in World War I, Charlie Chaplin, Coronations and various other great occasions as well as Christmas. Customized crackers were made for Britain's Royal Family, a tradition which continues to this day.

–LAURIE BELL

Poppets:

A Voodoo Doll by Any Other Name

MAKING POPPETS is a type of sympathetic magic dating back to prehistoric times. The gist of this kind of magical working is to direct energy onto an image or perform an action in order to create a desired result. For example, Stone Age hunters might have formed an image from the horns and skin of a deer, actually a primitive poppet, near a tribal fire while dancing around it pretending to "hunt" and "kill" the remains of the animal. The idea was that this drama would build an energy field to foreshadow a successful hunt in the future.

The first actual poppet might have appeared in ancient Egypt during the reign of Ramses III whose subjects detested him. Many hated this pharaoh enough to wish him dead and began to construct doll-like images of him which they could hang or burn. The intent, which has been consistent through the ages, was to use sympathetic magic. Thousands of years later in England, Guy Fawkes Day is celebrated to commemorate a failed plot to destroy the government by the infamous traitor. Images of that hated historical figure are still constructed of twigs and straw. These are then burned in large bonfires the night of November 5, the anniversary of his reprehensible act. The phrase "to burn in effigy" as a way of destroying someone in absentia reflects the sympathetic magic used to annihilate Guy Fawkes all over again. The destruction of his poppet suggests a wish that he burns on in the afterlife.

Usually linked with voodoo dolls, which are really poppets, the magical doll images have acquired a sinister reputation. Associated with mysterious Caribbean or African rituals, many believe they are used only to create a curse and cause harm. However this is far from the entire story. Poppets or voodoo dolls are used just as often for healing, prosperity and love rituals. The ancient Greeks created poppets called kollosos (pronounced 'caw law sauce'). When made in pairs and bound together the kollosos were intended to protect a love bond. The Greeks also used kollosos to bind and control dangerous ghostly spirits.

One thing is certain. Whether intended for good or not, poppets are extremely powerful tools for focusing spiritual energies toward a desired outcome. Poppets are portable. They can be made ahead of time, then carried easily by witches while on the move to be employed while at a comfortable distance from the intended target. These magical dolls can be fashioned from a variety of materials. Yarn, cloth, paper, sticks and straw, aluminum foil or clay are all good choices. Incorporating an appropriate stone, herbs or wax from a ritual candle burning into the poppet can further enhance the effectiveness of the sympathetic magic.

It's essential to concentrate on the intended subject while constructing the poppet. Speak its name aloud and talk to it. It isn't essential to be a great artist, just a basic figure resembling a human form will be fine. Some practitioners will incorporate a relic from the target into the poppet too. A relic is a personal physical link such as a hair, nail clipping, a scrap from an article of clothing or perhaps a small photograph.

A Witch from Germany once described how to make a protection poppet to halt an aggressive person. Her technique won't cause harm, but is merely intended to stop undesired contact. Once the image is complete, tie its arms close to the body, then place the doll in the freezer. Leave it there until the threat has passed. This puts the volatile situation "on ice," cooling the problem.

To make a love poppet, a piece of rose quartz might be inserted into the heart cavity of the doll. For healing try stuffing the poppet with a medicinal herb such as peppermint, which relieves pain and has been called the aspirin of the herb world. Green wax and a few coins or dollar bill would be appropriate for a poppet needed to attract money or improve a job related issue. Experiment, use colors and materials which feel comfortable and in harmony with the desired intent to you.

Once through with the doll, gently take it apart and bury or burn the remains. Don't use the same poppet for more than one person.

—SUE LEROY

⋛ Vine ⋚

Muin

CELTIC SCHOLARS now agree that the "vine" of the Druidic tree alphabet refers to the blackberry bramble bush. The sacred nature of the blackberry is evidenced in old tales and heathen customs observed down through the centuries. A loop of blackberry bramble served as a healing source in much the same way as a holed stone. Traditional rites involved passing baby through the loop three times to secure good health. One ancient legend tells how blackberries gathered and eaten within the span of the waxing moon at harvest time assured protection from the force of evil runes. For refuge in times of danger, one need only creep under a bramble bush. In rural regions of France and the British Isles, even to the present day, it is considered dangerous to eat blackberries. The reason given in Brittany is that the fruit belongs to the fairies and they resent it when mere mortals presume to taste the magical berries.

Blackberry is one of the few plants bearing blossoms and fruit at the same time. Its curative values were many and recognized in medieval herbals. A major virtue was its reputed power to lift the spirits by restoring energy and hope. This theme persisted, for in Victorian England physicians often prescribed blackberry cordial to cheer a depressed patient.

A clue to blackberry magic may be found in a nugget of country wisdom. When frozen dew covers blackberry blossoms at dawn in early spring, farmers rejoice and hail the event as a "blackberry winter." Without this frost, the berry will not set. What may appear threatening turns out to be a blessing, for the hoarfrost is a harbinger of a rich harvest.

Merry Meetings

A candle in the window, a fire on the hearth,
a discourse over tea...

ALTHOUGH THE WITCHES' ALMANAC staff normally conducts our interviews, this year we had the exciting opportunity to have David Conway interview Maxine Sanders for us. Since they have been friends for many years, this interview provides us with a unique display of conversation that could not be had between strangers. Thank you, David; and thank you, Maxine.

Much has changed since we both set out on our magical path in the nineteen-seventies. (Was it really more than forty years ago?) In those days magic was a minority interest. Nowadays one can't move without bumping into somebody who's into it. As for witchcraft and neo-paganism there seem to exist, at least to an outsider like me, more varieties on offer than Mr. Heinz's famous 57! Maxine, remind me what things were like when you started forth.

Well, David, in the 1960s there were far fewer covens. And of course secrecy was routinely observed so even those that existed contrived not to draw attention to themselves. This made sense as public attitudes to witchcraft were less tolerant than today. Most people knew about it only from what they'd read in the popular press. And journalists were only too happy to pander to their readers' fascination with sex and debauchery.

Indeed. As a small boy I remember seeing newspaper pictures of Gerald Gardner and two younger companions with their kit off. I seem to remember that Doreen Valiente fell out with him about so much, er, public exposure. She favoured discretion.

So did many of us. Our workings were simple, our trust in the magic unflinching, while our devotion to the Old Gods permitted no compromise. Like others I'd have been willing to die for the Craft and our right to practise it.

And Alex?

His devotion, too, was beyond question. But Alex was a complex, at times enigmatic, person. Today the word "charismatic" is used willy-nilly but I believe Alex was precisely that. He had about him—and no one knew it better than he—a quality, a kind of personal magnetism that drew people to him, foremost among them, of course, those eager to learn about witchcraft. Sadly, this same quality also had its downside. It's not that it went to his head, much as he relished the attention, but it did sometimes impair his judgement. This happened when the press got wind of him and sought to know more about what he was up to. And he, generous to

a fault, talked to them freely. The consequent publicity was not a great experience—here I understand Doreen's exasperation with Gardner—but Alex, bless him, thrived on it. No one relished media attention more than he did.

I've always supposed that what Alex set out to do was devise an alternative to the system which, whatever its claims to antiquity, had to have by and large been the invention of Gerald Gardner. Well of him and Doreen, whose contribution is sometimes overlooked. I have a vague notion of what Alex did differently but perhaps you can remind me.

I'll try. I must confess, however, that only recently have I got to know better the ways and workings of the Gardnerians. For a long time traditions other than our own—and there are of course several—never interested me greatly. But from what I've learned, it seems that some fundamental differences, both of emphasis and practice, do indeed exist.

One point worth making is that Alex recognised from the start that freedom, something he passionately believed in, depends always on choice. And for him the moment choice is withdrawn then freedom, too, goes with it. Such was his high regard for freedom that he sought never to compromise, let alone deny, an individual's right to choose to believe or to do this or that. Imposing his own preferences was not his way at all. I gather, however, that a similar respect for choice is not the case elsewhere.

Another difference concerns the practice of scourging. In our tradition, scourging takes place during Initiation and in certain other workings but never with any intention of causing pain or harm. Indeed, it was to discourage sado-masochists—and quite a few turned up on our doorstep—that Alex replaced the scourging thongs with silk ones.

After Initiation, nudity in Alexandrian craft becomes a matter of choice on all but a few occasions when certain types of magic are worked. (It's often more convenient, if nothing else, to be naked!) Offering a choice contradicts, so far as I understand it, the instruction in Doreen Valiente's version of the Charge. Yes, we do practise nudity but, as I said, for us it's usually a matter of choice not compulsion.

Our priority is to work magic. To that end our efforts are directed to attaining the shift in consciousness which allows one to experience—even in a sense "enter"—the numinous reality behind matter and form. It demands effort, hence our emphasis on training and self-discipline. We have a saying 'out of the worship comes the magic' and for us the worship that generates magic requires long, even arduous, practice. For that reason Alexandrians expect both self-discipline and sustained effort of their coven members.

We Alexandrians focus on the priesthood, on spirituality and on magic. Our joy—since we're not at all a gloomy bunch—comes first and foremost from the magic. (And yes, because we're only human, I must admit we sometimes stir the cauldron in more ways than one!) In addition we also go in for rather jolly Grand Sabbats, though the jollity doesn't compromise the more serious business of raising power or exploring together the theology and practice of Witchcraft.

What are relations like today between the Gardnerians and the Alexandrians? Do I discern a more ecumenical spirit than before, or are they still at loggerheads?

Nowadays the different traditions get on well enough. And so they should. That said there's a growing tendency to believe that initiation into the Craft means acceptance within a 'community,' one whose parts are all much of a muchness. Talk like that reminds me of the touchy-feely ecumenism popular among Christian denominations. Let's all be friends, certainly, but let's not pretend we're all one big happy-clappy family. I didn't seek Initiation with a view to joining a band of fellow

pilgrims, still less to improving my social life or adding names to my address book. My work as a priestess demands a lot of time and effort. It gives me little chance, even if I wanted it, to dally with people—mere hobbyists, some of them—who like to meet and talk about witchcraft. Good luck to them but please, count me out.

My impression—and I speak as an outsider—is that not all is love and light among the Alexandrians themselves. Indeed, I see that you yourself have come in for a lot of stick lately. What's that been all about?

The Alexandrian tradition rapidly fell victim to its own success. In no time at all we were inundated with requests for Initiation. And Alex, most generous but least discerning (let alone judgemental) of men, would say "Who am I to refuse?," then set about initiating all and too often, sundry. It turned out to be a mistake. The consequence has been too many initiates and too few teachers. Well, too few wise teachers, certainly.

One consequence of poor teaching has been a shift in emphasis from what I regard as essential—the Coven and its work—to the wider movement as such. A proliferation of social get-togethers, meetings and too many moots has, I feel, made the Craft mundane, quasi-secular and something it should never be—downright boring! Worse, these moots are often a device to win converts, something that has always been a no-no in the Craft. Better a few good and capable witches than a crowd who are neither. Too often today, I fear, the Craft is ill served by people whose am-

bitions are more mundane than magical, as well as by ill-informed teachers and, a new but noisy breed, the academically minded.

I am known, perhaps notorious, for saying what I mean. (And, I hope, for never saying what I don't.) I'd never question the right of others to disagree with me but disagreements should relate to matters of substance, not to the person whose views one disagrees with. Name-calling belongs to the playground, not to the Craft.

Hang on, you sound as if this is something you feel strongly about, something that's affected you personally.

It has. I expect my views to be challenged and make no claim to infallibility, but I'm saddened by the vituperation —it's not too strong a word—directed at me every now and then. And this just because my opinions chance to differ from those of my detractors. Not even someone as thick-skinned as I am can avoid being hurt from time to time. Hurt and disappointed. I don't want to cite examples—they're already out in the public domain—but I maintain that nothing is accomplished by attacking the singer because you happen not to like the song.

What saddens me—and again I speak as an outsider—is that thanks to the

126

Internet, differences are nowadays paraded like trophies, with little willingness to compromise or seek common ground. Of course there may sometimes be no common ground but in that case, one might hope for agreement to disagree without rancour or ill-feeling. Anyway before we stop and have a cup of tea—the brickies sort for you, I remember—let's hear a little more about the Alexandrian Craft. Tell me in a few words about its belief and practice.

Alexandrian Craft differs from other Traditions in several ways. We don't for instance keep the measure, taken at the 1st degree Initiation, while 2nd and 3rd degrees are given together. The 1st degree involves admission into the Mysteries, the 2nd penetration of the Mysteries and the 3rd their celebration. We do not use the scourge except at Initiation and as part of certain magical workings. Neither, as I pointed out, do we insist on nakedness other than at Initiation, while we seldom re-enact the mysteries, opting instead for direct access to them through magical workings. At all times Alexandrian initiates are free to come and go as their conscience dictates, although commitment and self-discipline are expected while they remain.

As for our Witch Queens, these retire in their late twenties, usually around twenty-eight. This is unrelated to notions of fertility, as might have been the case in ancient times, but to the fact that the priestess will by then have acquired a certain amount of knowledge, both occult and mundane, and with it the "tarnish" of ego. In other words, she has progressed to the Mother aspect and begun the process of nurturing the Child of Promise within her. No longer is she the Virgo Immaculata, the pure, untouched Maiden. That said, not all of today's groups observe this practice. On the contrary, human vanity being what it is, some Witch Queens hold on to the title for dear life.

Another characteristic of our Tradition is that we do not re-initiate unless the person applying to join our circle feels the need for it. We also insist on a 'no socialising rule' until candidates become Elders or gain access to the higher degrees. It has often struck me that if all Alexandrians stuck to this rule, much of the squabbling and rancour I discern nowadays would not have arisen. Which leads me to add that good manners, the outward sign of respect for others, are for me a requirement of all occultists. Equally important is the absence of mystery-mongering. Rarely will you hear an Alexandrian say "I can't tell you that because of my oath." No, mysteries are judiciously revealed to those who crave to understand.

One comfort, I suppose, is that disagreements, however unwelcome, are a sign of life, even vigour.

Since the nineteen-sixties when Alex burst onto to the scene, upsetting the elite— and elitist—high priesthood, Witchcraft of every hue has thrived. To this we owe in large part the rebirth of paganism, and the various groups that comprise it. To many it has brought immense joy and the freedom to worship in a way of their choosing, unfettered by the dogmas and moral strictures of orthodox religion.

Today I'm delighted that within contemporary Witchcraft, there seems agreement that good teachers are essential to its long-term survival. And the need for them is finally being met. It's been said that with maturity comes discernment. That, too, is now in evidence. Thanks to it, useless elements —embellishments that never lived up to their promise—are being seen for what they are and discarded. The Circle of the Wise has regained a wisdom it was at grave risk of losing.

Witchcraft is, as it was from the beginning, a vocation. If there's one lesson to be learned, it is that while many feel called, few, as the parable says, are fortunate enough to be chosen. The Craft is not elitist but being part of it requires qualities and commitment of a special kind. That's why it differs from the larger Pagan community, while still, as I'm the first to acknowledge, being a part of it. The truth remains, however, that attempts to make the Craft accessible to all—and we live in an egalitarian age—dilute the qualities that make and have always made Witchcraft not just

special but magical as well.

You sound optimistic about the future.

I'm confident that good manners, imagination and effective magical practice will ensure the future of the Craft. That said, each whole is only as good as its parts. Which is why I remain persuaded that the future of the Craft depends not on the wider community but on the work and commitment of those individual circles that comprise it. It's a case of small is beautiful and enduring.

Well, we've come a long way, the pair of us, from the Notting Hill Gate of the nineteen-seventies, you and Alex in Clanricarde Gardens and me, still a penniless student, around the corner in Portobello Road. We didn't know each other then, though we've worked out that we patronised the same launderette. (The machines, I remember, were pink and the dryer temperamental.) Oh dear, our youth has long gone. At least the magic stayed on.

Oh yes, I remember the launderette and the wonderful lady who ran it. We used regularly to chat about the world and its woes, or rather, how to right them. And all that while folding a pile of sweet-smelling freshly washed nappies.

As you say, the magic stayed. The two of us are still around to prove it!

Maxine Sanders' autobiography, Fire Child, *is available from Mandrake of Oxford (http://mandrake.uk.net/).*

David Conway's Magic: An Occult Primer *(new and revised edition) is available from the Witches' Almanac (http://thewitchesalmanac.com/books.html)*

Glossolalia—Speaking in Tongues

Languages of the Divine and Diabolical

THE SUPERNATURAL power of language is eloquently described by the famous Early American author. It is equally respected by those who would follow the path of the Witch in many ways. Chanting to manifest a desired result can evolve during the course of a ritual to become a string of syllables which assume a life of their own. Tongue twisters, tricky strings of words repeated several times rapidly, also mysteriously trip and tangle the original meaning. Immigrant non-English-speaking children often recount memories of attending kindergarten and not understanding a word the teacher was saying for weeks. Then, suddenly, the nonsense syllables became clear and they were able to speak and understand a new language, sometimes completely forgetting their mother tongue in the process.

These interesting but somewhat prosaic peculiarities hint at the deeper, hidden potentials and powers inherent in language. Among these is the controversial practice of speaking in tongues. The tongues are sounds which mimic the cadence of familiar conversation but are uttered, often in a trance state, in an unknown language.

> *Words—how potent for good or evil they become in the hands of one who knows how to combine them.*
> —Nathaniel Hawthorne

The technical term for this is glossolalia, from the Greek root words glossa (tongue) and lalia (to talk). There are three divisions within this mysterious phenomenon. There is the purest form of glossolalia, when neither the speaker nor the listener can make sense of the sounds. *Heteroglossolalia* occurs when an unfamiliar language is spoken but the listener hears it in his or her native tongue. *Xenoglossolalia* is when the speaker doesn't understand the language, but the hearer does.

Upon witnessing speaking in tongues, many questions can come to mind. Are the sounds spoken good or bad, of God or the Devil? Is it merely the imagination of the speaker at work? Is this an eccentric anomaly expressed by few or can anyone speak in tongues? Does this gift exist today or is it a shadow from the distant past?

Speaking in tongues may be rooted in the earliest religions of Asia and Africa where sorcerers would communicate mysterious and unintelligible words to their followers. Ancient Egyptian records tell of necromancers who uttered senseless noises which were thought to be messages from the gods. The historian Herodotus wrote of an inspired priest who suddenly spoke in a barbaric tongue. In *The Aeneid* Virgil also mentions a Sybil who spoke strangely and seemed spirit-possessed.

Detailed early documentation of speaking in tongues can be traced to the Oracle at Delphi in Greece around 400 B.C.E. In return for making a generous donation to the Temple of Apollo those seeking guidance could ask a single question of the Pythoness. She was a mystical being who would pray at a cracked altar poised above an earthquake fault. Soon she would begin a frenzied dance accompanied by a babble of incoherent utterances. A temple priest would translate what the Pythoness advised. She spoke in a sacred tongue which supposedly conveyed the direct words of Apollo. Many profound elements of Greek philosophy emerged from the Pythoness. "Know Thyself" is one which has been repeated often through the ages. Recently tests conducted on the air near the fissure have indicated that it emits toxic fumes.

The doctrine of the early Christian Church accepted glossolalia. By the 1800s the practice could be found among the Quakers, Shakers, Mormons, Methodists and Presbyterians. Although glossolalia is obviously not limited to Christianity, in contemporary times speaking in tongues is frequently associated with Pentecostal religious services. Believers claim they speak a heavenly language as a rule, although some tongues are demonic.

In 2006, Dr. Andrew Newberg of the University of Pennsylvania conducted a study of several people who spoke in tongues. This research was published in *The New York Times*. It was determined that brain imaging showed a number of changes taking place within the function of the brain. The test subjects were not in control of their usual language centers. While speaking in tongues, the frontal lobes of their brains—the part used to speak their native language—were completely quiet. This is consistent with the description the speakers gave of not being in intentional control. The faithful who support the authenticity of speaking in tongues took this University study as proof that the language of tongues is not fabricated and that it comes from a divine spiritual source.

Examples of glossolalia can be found among numerous non-Christian religions today. These include the Shamans of Greenland and Siberia, the Dyaks of Borneo, the Haida of the Pacific Northwest, the Zor Cult of Ethiopia, The Chako of South America and the Tibetan monks. Among Wiccans the November Eve Witches' Chant offers an intriguing example of the phenomenon of speaking in tongues.

Gerald Gardner, often hailed as "The Father of Modern Witchcraft," first published it in 1954 in his classic occult novel *High Magic's Aid*. Here is one version of The Witches' Chant. It has reappeared, with minor variations, in many rituals of power and invocations used by craft practitioners ever since.

> *Eko, eko, Azarak*
> *Eko, eko, Zomelak*
> *Bazabi lacha bachabe*
> *Lamac cahi achababe*
> *Karrellyos*
> *Lamac lamac Bachalyas*
> *Cabahagy sabalyos*
> *Baryolos*
> *Lagoz atha cabyolas*
> *Samahac atha famolas*
> *Hurrahya!*

There has been some speculation that the words are derived from Euskara, an ancient and complex language spoken by the Basques. Actually they have no clear translation, but more closely suggest that Gardner's chant is an example of glossolalia.

Summary of Behavioral Science Research Data on Glossolalia:

1. Glossolalia is an ancient and widespread phenomenon of most societies, occurring usually in connection with religion.

2. Glossolalia may occur as part of a larger condition of hysterical, dissociative, or trance states, or it may occur completely alone.

3. Glossolalia is not necessarily related to specific personality types.

4. Glossolalia may be deviant behavior due to abnormality of the mind, or it may be normal expected behavior, depending on the social and cultural environment.

5. Glossolalia is a form of partially developed speech in which the thought-speech apparatus of the person is used for a variety of internal mental functions.

6. Glossolalia may be a form of healthy regression in service of the ego, leading to more creative modes of life

–KATHRYN MUELLER

Fairy Beliefs in Rural France

"Saute haies, saute buissons,
Fais-moi aller où ils sont"

"Over bush, over bramble,
Take me to where they assemble"

SUCH AN INCANTATION did *La Sorcière*, "The Witch", chant over her broom before taking off to *Le Sabbat des Fées*, "The Fairy Sabbat."

In France, once homeland to the Gaulish tribes, folklore evolved into a rich assemblage of myths, legends and folktales inhabited by the "Fay" people whom the French call *Les Fées*.

The lore of French rural folk claims there was a time when *Le Petit Peuple*, "The Wee-Folk," thrived and found shelter amongst megalithic stone formations such as the alignments of Carnac in the Morbihan region of Brittany. They populated meadows, glades and sacred groves and inhabited foamy fountains. They entwined their voices to bubbling brooks and murmuring springs, haunted grottos and caves.

Ladies of the Grove

The most ancient of the Faye to drift across the passage of time were known as *Les Dames*, "The Ladies." Evocative of Druidesses, who for the ancient Celts were priestesses of a Cult rooted in antiquity, they became assigned to the role of nature deities indivisible from the mysteries of the forest, often seen dressed in flowing white robes and bearing a crown.

Back in Druidic times, Les Fées were more than likely powerful spirits of an otherworldly nature. They were seen to dwell in hollow mounds, sparkling waters and rushing winds, ministering the influence of divinities by the shades of deep forests, via the magical and medicinal knowledge of plants and by the emblems of sacred animals. Sound and dance were the primal art of their calling.

Besides roaming about to partake of Sabbats and Esbats, inhabitants of the Faerie Realms were reported to dwell in enchanted islands such as the mythic isle of Avalon, led by *la Fée Morgane*, guarding sacred orchards where fruits of immortality grew or on the Isle of Sein, near the coast of Brittany, an ancient Druidic burial ground.

During the Middle-Ages, Les Fées appeared as tall, fair and elegant women. Memories of their presence and subtle influence are still richly vivid in the 19th century, when the oral lore was first recorded. Once respected by folks at large, their activity seemingly starts to fade by the end of the 18th century. These miraculous creatures generally gifted with a good magical nature would later be known as destructive or malefic enchantresses due to the influence of the church.

Spinners of Destiny

The origin of the word *Fées* seems to come from the Latin feminine plural *Fata*, "The Fates;" and *Fari*, "To speak forth or utter a prophecy." Other possible sources are *Fatum* and *Fatantus*, "Destiny." *Fae* is found as an adjective as in *La Ronde Fae*, "the faery ring" or a verb as in Féer, "to enchant." The ideas of fate, prophecy and enchantment are intrinsically interwoven into the nature of the Fay.

Descendants of the Moirai from Greece, the Parcae from Rome were called *Tria Fata* and *Les Trois Fées*, "The Three Fairies." They spin the fabric of ordeals that anyone, by necessity, had to overcome or unravel while forging one's destiny, fatum, in the fires of transformation and skills. The Fatas were worshiped in groves of sacred trees, by rustling brooks and enchanted fountains. This cult from the Romans resonates with the Norse cult of the Norns. The Gaulish-Celtic lore of the Matres comes close, a triad of Celtic Mother-Goddesses associated with healing waters of fountains and sources, presiding over birth, fertility and abundance.

The first aspect of the Fatas spins the thread of life, and ties the knot of good wishes over newborns in witnessing their birth. She can foresee trends of future events and gifts the child accordingly. She is the ancestor of the good fairy godmother.

The second aspect of the Fatas, while extending the thread of life, will intervene in the life of mortals. As enchantress she influences the fate of humans with supernatural actions that may or may not be to one's advantage. Keeping the forces of life in equilibrium, she is an archetype of the Lady Magician.

The third aspect of the Fatas cuts the thread of life by announcing to humans their forthcoming death. Her role is one of psychopomp, guiding the spirit through other worlds towards a land of eternal youth. This aspect of *Fatas* became associated with darker and fearsome ideas related to forgotten knowledge. In some way they are the casting-mold for such figures as Maleficent in the *Legend of Sleeping Beauty*, *La Belle Dame sans Merci* drawing out life in the kiss of death. The same is true for Morgane Le Fay receiving Arthur on the Isle of Avalon when she was not leading false lovers to *Le Val sans Retour*, "The Perilous Vale."

Keepers of the Land

Although the word *Fées* is generally translated as Fairies, the *Lutin* or *Farfadet* was more like a dwarf, a sort of a crossbreed between an imp and a goblin. Not unlike the brownies of Scotland, Lutins, green or red caps, were known to play tricks and guard inaccessible treasures. Stone formations called *La Pierre qui Vire*, "The Spinning Stone," were believed to conceal the hollows where druidical golden sickles and charms were hidden, the access of which was only available during Yuletide when the stone would spin. As spirits associated to Yule, Lutins would guard such sites.

Terrestrial Fairies, *Les Margots*, when not attempting some mischief, kept good relations with humans, helping with finding names for newborn children, often blessing them with a "gift" (as a good fairy god-mother) and they could also foretell the future. *Les Mari-Morgan* were watery, sea-coast fairies. They were known of times to choose a young sailor as a lover, alluring him to dwell under water in a palace of purple, gold and of mother-of-pearl. The rich oral lore of Brittany survived secretly, in spite of an extremely harsh ban on traditional music and storytelling.

Les Bâtisseuses, "The Builders" were seen as giantesses who were responsible for dolmens, menhirs and megalithic stone formations. In later times they were also given the task of building castles and cathedrals. It is worth noting that many catholic cathedrals and monasteries were built over ancient Celtic sites of worship, themselves often set at the crossroads of Telluric forces. Such is Mount Saint-Michel built amongst the marshes on a

mound once sacred to Belenus, a solar fire and healing deity.

Les Lavandières were akin to the "Washers at the Ford" and were found at night by riverside and near fountains. Often pale and crone looking, they carried an otherworldly air about them that could send chills up the spine of stout hunters and thick-skinned farmers alike.

Les Dames Blanches, "The White Ladies," *Les Dames Vertes*, "The Green Ladies" and *Les Dames Rouges,* "The Red Ladies" were three distinct types. "The White Ladies" often appeared near or within the ruins of ancient castles. They predicted births and deaths. Some became protectors of family lineage while others were related to Les Lavandières. The Green Ladies were remembered in the East of France as lovely maidens seeking flowery glades and enchanted meadows but also as fierce guardians of sacred groves and of natural holy-healing springs. More scarce, The Red Ladies appeared near ravines and precipices protecting narrow paths that lead to hidden sacred sites. Once in a while, a foolish youth attempting to spy on the old ways of the Fay, found instead the threshold of death, unless favored by Les Dames Rouges, he was caught spellbound in an endless round, within the enchanted circle of a Full Moon Esbat. Concerning The Green Ladies and The Red Ladies, the author is inclined to think they were two-thirds of this world and one-third of the Fay.

Certainly the most elusive and dangerous amongst Les Fées were *Les Vouivres* whose appearance was as winged serpents with a jewel on the forehead, a vestment they could secretly cast off, so to bathe and dance as lovely naiads. It is said that amongst the Vouivres, the most popular certainly was *La Fée Mélusine*, attached to the House of Lusignan in Poitou, who was believed to be part Vouivre and part Dame Blanche.

Spirits Calling

Go out at twilight or midnight to wander by the countryside and if you can, find some ancestral oak in a quiet glade, seek out the song in the bubbling waters of a nearby spring, watch the remnants of standing stones ghostly silhouetted against a hazy sky. You may feel a slight vertigo enticing you towards a round of revelry as once was danced upon the green. Know there and then that Les Fées, Les Dames, Les Lutins are never very far, and while they may seem to dwell in some otherworld, Le Petit Peuple and Les Follets are ever eager to witness and to assist, if called forth with appropriate offerings, due respect and fair enchantment.

—GWALCHTAN

Corpse Doors

OUR DISTANT ancestors employed numerous methods to keep the dead from returning to haunt the living. In Ireland, though a window was opened at the time of death to let the spirit leave, it was closed after a short time so the spirit could not re-enter. The Navajo didn't take any chances. They collapsed and abandoned the hogan in which a person died.

The Norse worried that if a corpse faced the house while being removed, it would see which house it came from and would be able to find its way back, so they carried corpses out of the house feet first.

They were especially fearful of the return of the dead, for it was believed they could return as draugar, undead creatures who possessed supernatural strength. Destroying a draug (singular) was nasty business. In addition to supernatural strength, the draugar possessed the ability to increase their size at will, making it a formidable opponent. Because the draugar was so hard to kill, they considered it wiser to prevent the transformation than to exterminate the result.

Sacred Rites

When a person died, the Norse followed strict protocol. They would lay a pair of open scissors on the dead person's chest and small pieces of straw crosswise under the shroud. The scissors, being iron or steel, would be imbued with the magical powers of the metal. In an open position they formed the shape of a cross, as did the pieces of straw. This invoked the protection of the Christian cross. The protocol contained a third invocation of the powers of Christian belief. Just within the threshold of the door, as the coffin was carried out, the bearers raised and lowered it three times in different directions, forming a cross.

To prevent the corpse from walking if it did wake, the family would tie the big toes together and also stick needles in the sole of the feet. The needles, also being of iron or steel, would have magical properties in addition to the practical value of causing pain to the revenant.

Yet the most effective way of preventing a draug was to use a corpse door. The family would open a hole in the wall of the house. With mourners standing close around the coffin to block the view, the bearers would carry the corpse feet first through this door. While the family processed to the place of burial, others would stay behind, bricking up the door so that the corpse could not use it to return, for they believed the dead could only return the way they left.

Hidden Portals

As late as 1907 there was still evidence of this practice. A folklorist returning to the west coast of Jutland reported seeing the outline of what he thought was a bricked-up oven door on the gable-end of a house. It didn't make sense to him since the wall was the outer wall of the house's "best room" or "company room" and one wouldn't be baking there. When he asked the inhabitants what it was, they told him it was a corpse door. Though not in use at that time, it was still alive in local memory.

Even now, the Draugr lives on in memory, though in video games, novels and graphic novels. Examples include The Elder Scrolls series of action role-playing games, The Morganville Vampire young adult urban fantasy novels from Rachel Caine, as well as The Corpse Door by Kris Sayer.

–MORVEN WESTFIELD

Doll-in-the-Grass

ONCE UPON A TIME a certain king had a certain whim. Kings do tend to have whims and sometimes, now-and-then, once-in-a-blue-moon the whims are reasonable. This particular whim began reasonably enough. When his twelve sons were grown, the king decreed they should go into the world and find themselves wives. But he commanded also that each bride must be able to weave, spin and sew a shirt in a day or he would not have her for a daughter-in-law. Who can fathom the profound mind of kings?

The monarch wished his sons good spouse questing and gave each prince a horse and a coat of mail. The princes set out together and had gone some distance when they declared that they would not allow Boots, the youngest brother, to quest with them. "You are a good-for-nothing, fit for nothing," they told him. "Princes are the superstars of the realm and you just embarrass your royal kin." And to put it as kindly as possible, we have to report with some sorrow that Boots was indeed a bit of a simpleton.

The young prince, abandoned at the roadside by his brothers, was shattered. He had no idea what to do or where to go next. Boots dismounted, sat down in the tall grass and wept in confusion. Suddenly tufts of grass rustled, stirred, and there appeared a charming miniature of a girl. Boots was astounded. "Would you like to come with me and meet Doll-in-the-Grass?" she asked. Overcome with curiosity, Boots agreed.

The odd couple

Doll-in-the-Grass was sitting on a chair of fragrant rosemary, wearing a dress woven of violets. She was a figure as big as your thumb, as beautiful as a summer morning, as smart as ten professors in a row. "Why are you weeping?" she asked. Boots told her his brothers had forsaken him at roadside and that he was in quest of a bride that could spin, weave and sew a shirt in a day. "If you can do that, it will be my happiness to make you my wife," he declared, dazzled by her lovely form, tiny as it was. Did I mention that what Boots lacked in brains he embodied in heart? Doll-in-the-Grass recognized the loving nature of the prince and agreed. At a dizzying speed she spun, she wove and she sewed a perfect little shirt with buttons so small as to be invisible, for the shirt was only the size of half a thumb.

Boots set off with it back to the castle, apprehensive of what his father would think of the shirtlet. But the king chuckled at the charm and wit of the garment and gave his permission for his son to wed its maker, however odd her size. Boots returned at a gallop, thrilled to claim his little sweetheart and bring her back to the castle as his bride.

The couple rejoiced at their meeting, and the prince tried to scoop her up to ride before him on his saddle. But Doll-in-the-Grass insisted on her own way to go. "I have my own carriage and horses," she said proudly. The "carriage" was a silver spoon, the "horses" little white mice with reins of silken thread. Boots rode on the opposite side of the road, fearful of crushing his bride, she was so little.

Eleven ugly brides

When they came to a river, Boots's horse, spooked by the water, reared and upset the spoon. Doll-in-the-Grass was hurled into the water and sank. Boots plunged into the river and fished around, hoping to find her and pull her out. But he found no trace of his beloved and finally threw himself down on the river bank in shock, heartbroken. Suddenly the water roiled and a merman surfaced with a lady in his arms—Doll-in-the-Grass, wet, shiny, of human size and lovelier now than ever. The merman waved his tail and vanished.

Boots took his bride up on his saddle and rode home with her. All his brothers had returned with their ugly brides who had been quarreling all the way home. Each carried an ill-made shirt already falling apart at the seams. When his brothers saw Boots's beautiful bride, they burst with jealousy and began to attack him. The king was so dismayed at his nasty new family that he drove away the eleven brothers and eleven brides and destroyed the eleven raggedy shirts. He gave Boots and Doll-in-the-Grass a beautiful wedding feast. Then, the old Norse tale assures us, "they lived well and happily together a long, long time, and if they're not dead, why, they're alive still."

—BARBARA STACY

Adapted from Popular Tales from the Norse, by Peter Christen Asbjornsen and Jorgen Moe.

EASTER WITCHES

IN THE UNITED STATES, the non-religious and religious alike celebrate Easter by coloring eggs and setting up baskets to receive candy and gifts from the Easter Bunny. In Finland and Sweden though, you're more likely to find Easter Witches, and they're getting candy, not giving it.

Little girls dress up as witches (påskkärring) in a brightly colored kerchief, shawl and long skirt. Often they carry a broom. Their costumes may be either tattered or new, and some wear conical witch hats instead of the traditional triangular piece of cloth tied around the head. They rouge their cheeks and freckle their nose and face, making them resemble a Raggedy Ann doll more than a folkloric witch.

Like American children on Halloween, the Easter Witches go door-to-door gathering candy from their neighbors which they collect in wicker baskets or copper teapots. Carrying sprigs of pussy willow decorated with spring-colored feathers and crepe paper, they exchange the twigs for candy while reciting this traditional rhyme:

Virvon, varvon, tuoreeks terveeks,
tulevaks vuodeks;
vitsa sulle, palkka mulle!

The translation:

I wave a twig for a fresh and healthy
year ahead;
a twig for you, a treat for me!

Pussy willow branches have long been

a symbol of spring and in some cultures where palms do not grow natively, pussy willows are blessed on Palm Sunday instead. In Sweden, twigs of birch, not pussy willow, are decorated with colored feathers at Easter.

The pussy willows that grow in northern Europe are the goat willow (*Salix caprea*), also called goat sallow and the grey willow (*Salix cinerea*), also called grey sallow. Like the American pussy willow (*Salix discolor*), the male catkins of these trees go through a fuzzy stage where they look like tiny kittens before they burst into flower, giving them the nickname pussy willow.

So why are there witches at Easter? Tradition says that in ancient times, witches travelled on Maundy Thursday (the Thursday before Easter) to Blåkulla, which was either a physical place (one tradition sets it on an island) or an astral destination, to worship the devil. Some even think that Blåkulla was the Brocken in Germany (see *Walpurgisnacht*, Issue 34, Spring 2015 to Spring 2016 of The Witches' Almanac).

One part of the tradition says that bonfires were lit to scare away the witches as they flew over land on their way to their destination and bonfires still play a part in the Easter celebration. The pussy willows and other signs of spring are to welcome the season and make light of what was feared (witches).

–MORVEN WESTFIELD

THE PLEIADES

Seven Mysterious Sisters

THE PLEIADES is unique in that it is prominent in the cosmology of nearly every culture. Highly conspicuous in the night sky, the Pleiades is actually a cluster of at least seven separate stars. Various traditions portray them as seven sisters, hens or maidens. They are grouped within one degree of longitude of each other, so for interpretation purposes they are always read together. Alcyone, the principal and brightest star in the cluster, is the reference point. The others are Maia, Electra, Taygete, Celaeno, Sterope and Merope (who is said to be the lost or missing Pleiad and is invisible except to those with exceptional eyesight). Sometimes two more stars are added to represent their parents, Atlas and Pleione.

The legends of what the Pleiades are and whether they are considered positive or negative vary greatly between cultures. One Native American legend links them to unloved orphans who retreated to the sky to mourn and lament, while in the

Baltic countries, especially Latvia and Lithuania, they become a group of sisters walking to their weddings, escorted by a benevolent brother. The esoteric astrology of the Theosophical Society presents the Pleiades as a focusing of the seven rays uplifting humanity. Various New Age writers have related Pleiades to spiritual transformations following a cataclysm. The stars are seen as messengers for human destiny.

In medieval times star diagrams were used in ritual magic. Today such a diagram appears on a vehicle. The Pleiades is the emblem for the Japanese-made Subaru. The popular auto's name means Pleiades in Japanese. Although the manufacturer says the official choice of the star cluster emblem is symbolic of the merging of several Japanese companies, there might be a more subtle and mystical meaning.

The Pleiades are of special interest at present because of a rare sign change.

The star cluster, which has been read throughout the history of modern astrology as being in the sign of Taurus, has just entered 00 degrees of Gemini 00 minutes. Since the fixed stars move only a single degree every 72 years or so, a sign change like this occurs about once every 2160 years. Filtered through the characteristics of Gemini, the Pleiades' influences can begin to operate on a very different level. There is no precedent for this, so it provides a marvelous opportunity for astrological research. During the year to come transit Mars will conjoin the Pleiades April 18–25, 2017. The potentials of this potent star cluster will influence both world events and personal situations at that time.

–DIKKI-JO MULLEN

(See our website thewitchesalmanac.com under the Almanac Extras section for more information about the specifics of interpreting the Pleiades.)

Mother Winter's Antlers

MANY PAGANS the world over talk about The Earth Mother and Horned Father in terms of the Moon Goddess and the Sun God. One wheel of the year story is that of the Goddess giving birth to the Sun God, who grows alongside the plants of spring. At the Great Rite of Beltane the pair conceive a child as the God reaches adulthood. He dies at Hallows and the Goddess carries their child until Yule, when she gives birth to the Sun God again and the cycle continues. Birth, Death, Rebirth. In each cycle the Mother, the Great Goddess, carries her child within her and gives him unto the world in the middle of winter at Yule, the longest night. She brings this present to the world year after year.

And yet there is little known in the way of Mother Winter. Instead, we turn towards Father Winter, with his beard so snowy white. He is the consort of the Queen of the Wood, who herself is a faye. Children look to Santa, with his pack of male reindeer to deliver their gifts each Christmas. Many often look to the God, the Horned One, as the one who will carry the Sun in his antlers back to the people, bringing warmth, rejuvenation and new crops in spring. This imagery is seen in many places, the stag with the sun in his antlers. Or is it?

What if that snowy beard was actually Mother Winter, the Crone, with her long flowing white hair coming across the frozen lands of the north? What if that stag we are so familiar with was actually a doe? We talk of the crone, the wise woman, the giver of knowledge. But who is she and where does she reside? It would make sense for her to live at the farthest reaches of the Earth. In the frozen North perhaps, where she shakes out her feather bed, as in the story of "Mother Winter's Visit," bringing snow and rain to the land

Continuing with Mother Winter residing in the snowy north, it would stand to reason that a reindeer would carry the Sun in his antlers. Only, the male reindeer drop their antlers in early December, weeks before the Winter Solstice, when the Sun would be returning to the people. The female deer, the mother of the winter lands, is the one who would be left with antlers to carry the newborn Sun. The Goddess, in the form of a doe, bringing the greatest gift there is, hope and renewal when the world is clothed in darkness most of the day.

In pre-Christian times, Reindeer Mothers were venerated as the Great Goddess herself. Priestesses were depicted with antlers on their heads. Stories passed along orally spoke of a horned Mother Goddess giving birth to both deer and human children alike. Snowy realms abound throughout northern Eurasia, where many Pagan religions find their shadowy origins. In Mongolia, monoliths called "deer stones" stand and are decorated with stylized depictions of deer jumping and leaping as if in flight. In Hungary, deer are also associated with the celestial. There are paintings of a Tree of Life sprouting out of a deer skull like a pair of antlers, entwined and holding the Sun and Moon above.

Even today, shaman women in Siberia dress in traditional garb and ride through the snow in sleds pulled by reindeer. In the mountains it is believed the reindeer and shamans eat a particular type of mushroom and actually fly. The mushroom ingested is red with white spots and their garments are red trimmed in white, similar to those attributed to Santa. This may be the origin of tales of Santa's reindeer flying through the night sky with him.

This year, as the nights lengthen and darkness wraps its quiet arms about the world, consider this. Solstice will come with its revelry and ritual. The hope of the world is coming. The life giving force, the greatest present the world can receive will be delivered. The world around us heralds it in, whether through Yule or Christmas or another festival of light. The Sun shall return as it has year after year. But who is carrying Him? Perhaps Great Mother Winter in the form of a doe, carrying the Sun in her antlers.

–HELIE

SIR ARTHUR CONAN DOYLE

Explorer, Author and Spiritualist

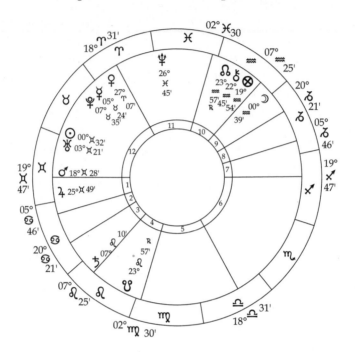

ALTHOUGH his name usually brings to mind Sherlock Holmes, the eccentric and brilliant detective character he created, Sir Arthur Conan Doyle was also an enthusiastic advocate of afterlife communication and psychic phenomena. Born in Edinburgh, Scotland on May 22, 1859, at 4:55 a.m. into a middle-class family, he epitomized the sunshine of the British Empire, the times of Queen Victoria and King Edward VII.

A well spoken, confident and tall gentleman, Doyle was true to the dual and multi-faceted nature of Gemini, his birth sign. An avid reader from childhood on, he studied abroad in Austria. After graduation from the University of Edinburgh medical school he sought excitement by sailing to the Arctic as a ship's doctor. This was almost too much of an adventure. After fighting off a shark, a fire aboard the vessel and typhoid fever, he returned home barely alive. Resolving to stay safely on dry land, Doyle opened a medical practice in Portsmouth, England.

Born on the cusp of Taurus with his Sun at 0 degrees Gemini, great complexity of character is indicated. While he was a pragmatic scientist and physician, he was also a talented storyteller. His Sun was conjunct Uranus, showing originality and an affinity for the occult. Doyle was a double Gemini with his ascendant (rising sign) also being in the sign of the Twins. Mars in Gemini is rising, conjunct the ascendant and Jupiter. The Mars-Jupiter conjunction promises a magnanimous personality. The benevolent fixed star Rigel (associated with honors and riches) is located near his natal Mars, ascendant and Jupiter. This all combines enough assertiveness and motivation to impact the world. Throughout his life, A. Conan Doyle gained much knowledge and wisdom through his many experiences. His Saturn was in Leo in the 3rd house, showing pride and dignity as well as an urge to share thoughtful, meaningful communication.

By 1891 he gave up practicing medicine to write full time. His Mercury was conjunct Pluto in Taurus, showing persistence and depth of thought as well as a love of music. It was Doyle's detective stories in the form of *The Adventures of Sherlock Holmes* which catapulted him to fame, earning an untold income along the way.

His life suddenly crumbled into chaos when Doyle's beloved first wife Louise developed tuberculosis and died. Kingsley, his oldest son, perished too. With six placements in his 12th house, the section of the horoscope related to disappointments, secrets, institutions and sorrows, Doyle was prone to depression, nightmares and mood swings. His life was punctuated by extremes of both joy and tragedy. His father's alcoholism and eventual mental illness shadowed him from childhood on.

It was following these many setbacks that he joined the Society For Psychical Research and embraced

the study of the paranormal. He had Venus in Aries which often indicates an affinity for the military. Doyle felt drawn to serve his country as a medical doctor. After volunteering for service in the Royal Army during the Boer War, he was knighted in 1902 by Edward VII. At that highlight in his life Jupiter was transiting Aquarius, conjunct his natal Moon and transit Pluto was in Gemini, conjunct his ascendant.

Following World War I Doyle's second wife, Jean, joined him in his efforts to reunite bereaved families with the spirits of beloved husbands, fathers and brothers who had been killed in battle. Neptune in Pisces in the 11th house describes his confused and mixed experiences with unusual social contacts. Among these was the famed magician Harry Houdini, who was Doyle's good friend but later became a bitter enemy following an argument regarding a séance.

Doyle's Moon was at 0 degrees of Aquarius in the disseminating phase, indicating an inventive and liberal nature. The Moon was also exactly trine his Gemini Sun, a very fortunate aspect blessing him with luck as well as recuperative powers. The Part of Fortune, Chiron and Moon's north node were also in Aquarius, underscoring his interest in humanity and psychology. The Aquarius placements spanned the 9th and 10th houses. This indicates notoriety, a stellar career, intellectual prowess and foreign travel. Sir Arthur and Lady Doyle traveled to the United States, where they were wildly popular, as well as Europe, New Zealand, South Africa and Australia. Their lectures involved afterlife experiences and evidence of paranormal phenomena. Doyle wrote extensively about these topics during the early 20th century.

In later life he held nightly séances at his home and supported a psychic bookshop, lending library and museum. Sir Arthur Conan Doyle passed into spirit on July 7, 1930. A few days later on July 13 the famed medium Estelle Roberts gave messages which the family validated from "the old fighter," as Doyle was nicknamed, at a memorial reception where an empty chair had been left for him.

–DIKKI-JO MULLEN

Poster for the 1900 play
Sherlock Holmes by Conan Doyle
and actor William Gillette

SIR ARTHUR CONAN DOYLE
Born May 22, 1859
at 4:55 a.m. UT in Edinburgh, Scotland

Data Table
Tropical Placidus Houses

Sun 00 Gemini 32 – 12th house

Moon 00 Aquarius 39 – 9th house

(waning Moon in the disseminating phase)

Mercury 05 Taurus 24 – 12th house

Venus 27 Aries 07 – 12th house

Mars 18 Gemini 28 – 12th house (rising)

Jupiter 25 Gemini 49 – 1st house

Saturn 07 Leo 10 – 3rd house

Uranus 03 Gemini 21 – 12th house

Neptune 26 Pisces 45 – 11th house

Pluto 07 Taurus 35– 12th house

Chiron 22 Aquarius 45 – 10th house

North Node of the Moon (true node) 23 Aquarius 57 – 10th house

Part of Fortune 19 Aquarius 54 – 10th house

Ascendant (rising sign) is 19 Gemini 47

Sleeping With Water
Somnambulant Imbibing

THE SACRED, holy and life-giving properties of water have long been revered and observed by those who follow the old ways. Legendary wells with miraculous powers such as the Chalice Well in Glastonbury, England, and the Fountain of Youth in St. Augustine Florida, are present around the world. In the Bahamas the Island of Bimini has a sacred well which has been linked with healing powers. The same is true of Aguas Calientes ("hot water" in Spanish). This Peruvian village located at the base of Machu Picchu is named for its sacred water.

Cherished waters retrieved from a sacred source credited with special attributes can be used in a number of ways. Washing, drinking or house blessings might come to mind. However one of the most effective and less familiar techniques is that of sleeping with water. Happily, this simple but effective technique can be used with either a sacred water or with regular tap water to which a teaspoon or so of salt has been added. The crystals in the salt will act as a catalyst to release the water's inherent powers.

At night upon retiring, fill a favorite glass, cup or chalice with a few ounces of water and place it beside the bed. The water will attract and hold any undesirable vibrations or negative energy which might be afoot, protecting the vulnerable sleeper. In the morning upon awakening the water is immediately discarded, either poured down the drain or outside the door. Do not drink it. Adopted as a regular ritual each night, sleeping with water has been known to enhance physical well-being and peace of mind.

If visiting a sacred site for water isn't an option and something more than regular tap water seems appealing, here are other water sources which also have unique characteristics. These can be considered when selecting water to try this nightly blessing or other ritual uses.

Sea Water

All of the world's oceans with their naturally occurring salt and minerals fall into this category. King Solomon, a holy figure appearing in several spiritual traditions claimed God communicated to him that the sea would attract and absorb any evil thing. Try to collect sea water at the incoming tide.

River Water

Continuous motion forward, defining of boundaries and the virtue of looking toward the future while releasing the past is the energy carried.

Spring Water

Coming from underground, this water brings a penetrating and assertive quality.

Rain Water

A variable energy is present. It provides a connection to current events and being a part of activities related to the mass consciousness. It brings a closer attunement with associates and the surroundings.

Lake Water

A serene and gentle vibration is present here. Stability, receptivity and a freshness is present with lake water.

Holy Water

This is the name given to ordinary water which has been blessed in a Catholic or Episcopal Church by an ordained priest. It is also water especially blessed by other initiates including shamans, high priests or priestesses for ritual work. Usually table salt is added to ordinary water and a prayer is said, dedicating the water and salt to sacred practices. Often a small vial of holy water is carried in a vehicle, pocket or purse for protection. Use holy water while praying to invoke a blessing. It can be sprinkled in a home or around a dinner table for protection or added to bath water.

Sprinkle Water

This is water intended to sprinkle around a dwelling or other building to drive away undesired forces. It can also be used in the practice of sleeping with water. Sprinkle water is any water that has had herbs steeped in it so that properties of the plants will combine with the qualities of the water.

Here are some effective herbs often used in preparing sprinkle water:

Yarrow—romantic love

Sage—clarity and protection

Rue—spiritual awakening and inner peace

Mint—a new home, healing and energizing

Basil—prosperity and strength to face challenges

—MARINA BRYONY

The Thistle's Experiences

BELONGING to the lordly manor-house was a beautiful, well-kept garden, with rare trees and flowers; the guests of the proprietor declared their admiration of it; the people of the neighborhood, from town and country, came on Sundays and holidays, and asked permission to see the garden; indeed, whole schools used to pay visits to it.

Outside the garden, by the palings at the road-side, stood a great mighty Thistle, which spread out in many directions from the root, so that it might have been called a thistle bush. Nobody looked at it, except the old Ass which drew the milk-maid's cart. This Ass used to stretch out his neck towards the Thistle, and say, "You are beautiful; I should like to eat you!" But his halter was not long enough to let him reach it and eat it.

There was great company at the manor-house—some very noble people from the capital; young pretty girls, and among them a young lady who came from a long distance. She had come from Scotland, and was of high birth, and was rich in land and in gold—a bride worth winning, said more than one of the young gentlemen; and their lady mothers said the same thing.

The young people amused themselves on the lawn, and played at ball; they wandered among the flowers, and each of the young girls broke off a flower, and fastened it in a young gentleman's buttonhole. But the young Scotch lady looked round, for a long time, in an undecided way. None of the flowers seemed to suit her taste. Then her eye glanced across the paling—outside stood the great thistle bush, with the reddish-blue, sturdy flowers; she saw them, she smiled, and asked the son of the house to pluck one for her.

"It is the flower of Scotland," she said. "It blooms in the scutcheon of my country. Give me yonder flower."

And he brought the fairest blossom, and pricked his fingers as completely as if it had grown on the sharpest rose bush.

She placed the thistle-flower in the buttonhole of the young man, and he felt himself highly honored. Each of the other young gentlemen would willingly have given his own beautiful flower to have worn this one, presented by the fair hand of the Scottish maiden. And if the son of the house felt himself honored, what were the feelings of the Thistle bush? It seemed to him as if dew and sunshine were streaming through him.

"I am something more than I knew of," said the Thistle to itself. "I suppose my right place is really inside the palings, and not outside. One is often strangely placed in this world; but now I have at least managed to get one of my people within the pale, and indeed into a buttonhole!"

The Thistle told this event to every blossom that unfolded itself, and not many days had gone by before the Thistle heard, not from men, not from the twittering of the birds, but from the air itself, which stores up the sounds, and carries them far around—out of the most retired walks of the garden, and out of the rooms of the house, in which doors and windows stood open, that the young gentleman who had received the thistle-flower from the hand of the fair Scottish maiden had also now received the heart and hand of the lady in question. They were a handsome pair—it was a good match.

"That match I made up!" said the Thistle; and he thought of the flower he had given for the buttonhole. Every flower that opened heard of this occurrence.

"I shall certainly be transplanted into the garden," thought the Thistle, and perhaps put into a pot, which crowds one in. That is said to be the greatest of all honors."

And the Thistle pictured this to himself in such a lively manner, that at last he said, with full conviction, "I am to be transplanted into a pot."

Then he promised every little thistle flower which unfolded itself that it also

153

should be put into a pot, and perhaps into a buttonhole, the highest honor that could be attained. But not one of them was put into a pot, much less into a buttonhole. They drank in the sunlight and the air; lived on the sunlight by day, and on the dew by night; bloomed—were visited by bees and hornets, who looked after the honey, the dowry of the flower, and they took the honey, and left the flower where it was.

"The thievish rabble!" said the Thistle. "If I could only stab every one of them! But I cannot."

The flowers hung their heads and faded; but after a time new ones came.

"You come in good time," said the Thistle. "I am expecting every moment to get across the fence."

A few innocent daisies, and a long thin dandelion, stood and listened in deep admiration, and believed everything they heard.

The old Ass of the milk-cart stood at the edge of the field-road, and glanced across at the blooming thistle bush; but his halter was too short, and he could not reach it.

And the Thistle thought so long of the thistle of Scotland, to whose family he said he belonged, that he fancied at last that he had come from Scotland, and that his parents had been put into the national escutcheon. That was a great

thought; but, you see, a great thistle has a right to a great thought.

"One is often of so grand a family, that one may not know it," said the Nettle, who grew close by. He had a kind of idea that he might be made into cambric if he were rightly treated.

And the summer went by, and the autumn went by. The leaves fell from the trees, and the few flowers left had deeper colors and less scent. The gardener's boy sang in the garden, across the palings:

"Up the hill, down the dale we wend,
That is life, from beginning to end."

The young fir trees in the forest began to long for Christmas, but it was a long time to Christmas yet.

"Here I am standing yet!" said the Thistle. "It is as if nobody thought of me, and yet I managed the match. They were betrothed, and they have had their wedding; it is now a week ago. I won't take a single step-because I can't."

A few more weeks went by. The Thistle stood there with his last single flower large and full. This flower had shot up from near the roots; the wind blew cold over it, and the colors vanished, and the flower grew in size, and looked like a silvered sunflower.

One day the young pair, now man and wife, came into the garden. They went along by the paling, and the young wife looked across it.

"There's the great thistle still growing," she said. "It has no flowers now."

"Oh, yes, the ghost of the last one is there still," said he. And he pointed to the silvery remains of the flower, which looked like a flower themselves.

"It is pretty, certainly," she said. "Such a one must be carved on the frame of our picture."

And the young man had to climb across the palings again, and to break off the calyx of the thistle. It pricked his fingers, but then he had called it a ghost. And this thistle-calyx came into the garden, and into the house, and into the drawing-room. There stood a picture—"Young Couple." A thistle-flower was painted in the buttonhole of the bridegroom. They spoke about this, and also about the thistle-flower they brought, the last thistle-flower, now gleaming like silver, whose picture was carved on the frame.

And the breeze carried what was spoken away, far away.

"What one can experience!" said the Thistle Bush. "My first born was put into a buttonhole, and my youngest has been put in a frame. Where shall I go?"

And the Ass stood by the road-side, and looked across at the Thistle.

"Come to me, my nibble darling!" said he. "I can't get across to you."

But the Thistle did not answer. He became more and more thoughtful— kept on thinking and thinking till near Christmas, and then a flower of thought came forth.

"If the children are only good, the parents do not mind standing outside the garden pale."

"That's an honorable thought," said the Sunbeam. "You shall also have a good place."

"In a pot or in a frame?" asked the Thistle.

"In a story," replied the Sunbeam.

—HANS CHRISTIAN ANDERSEN

Moon Cycles

A New Moon rises with the Sun,
Her waxing half at midday shows,
The Full Moon climbs at sunset hour,
And waning half the midnight knows.

NEW	2018	FULL	NEW	2019	FULL
January 16		January 1, 31*	January 5		January 21
February 15		No full moon	February 4		February 19
March 17		March 1, 31*	March 6		March 20
April 15		April 29	April 5		April 19
May 15		May 29	May 4		May 18
June 13		June 28	June 3		June 17
July 12		July 27	July 2, 31**		July 16
August 11		August 26	August 30		August 15
September 9		September 24	September 28		September 14
October 8		October 24	October 27		October 13
November 7		November 23	November 26		November 12
December 7		December 22	December 26		December 12

* Blue Moons on January 31, 2018 and March 31, 2018
** July 31 A rare second New Moon in the same month is called a Black Moon, Occurring on July 31, 2019, it is sacred to the fey ones

Life takes on added dimension when you match your activities to the waxing and waning of the Moon. Observe the sequence of her phases to learn the wisdom of constant change within complete certainty.

Dates are for Eastern Standard and Daylight Time.

presage

by Dikki-Jo Mullen

ARIES, 2017–PISCES, 2018

ANOTHER JOURNEY through the zodiac begins with the Vernal Equinox. Fiery sunlight melts the remaining winter's snow and life is renewed. As plants blossom and baby birds hatch, nature's energetic zest for life presages a new phase for humanity. Shimmering veils of celestial energies subtly emitted by heavenly bodies stream to Earth to shape the year ahead.

Presage interprets this for you. Begin with your familiar birth or Sun sign, the most significant forecast; it describes how you shine. The forecast for your Moon sign explores emotions. Your ascendant (rising sign) will describe the tangible self, appearance and interaction with the world around you.

Flowers for each zodiac sign are included in reference to the May Day holiday. Flowers are powerful, beau-

tiful sources of positive energy. They can be added to improve and uplift your surroundings. The Tarot provides a key to understanding astrology as well as alchemy, numerology and the entire spectrum of the human experience. A Tarot card linked to each zodiac sign is included in the Spirituality sections.

Until October 10 Jupiter transits Libra. This emphasizes growth regarding legal and social boundaries. Near the Winter Solstice Saturn enters Capricorn, where it will join Pluto. This addresses economic realities, earth changes and agriculture. The four eclipses this year are in Leo and Aquarius. They promise to bring the unexpected regarding creativity, entertainment, young people, technology and humanitarian issues.

Here begins Presage, your guidebook for navigating the year to come.

ASTROLOGICAL KEYS

Signs of the Zodiac
Channels of Expression

ARIES: fiery, pioneering, competitive
TAURUS: earthy, stable, practical
GEMINI: dual, lively, versatile
CANCER: protective, traditional
LEO: dramatic, flamboyant, warm
VIRGO: conscientious, analytical
LIBRA: refined, fair, sociable
SCORPIO: intense, secretive, ambitious
SAGITTARIUS: friendly, expansive
CAPRICORN: cautious, materialistic
AQUARIUS: inquisitive, unpredictable
PISCES: responsive, dependent, fanciful

Elements

FIRE: Aries, Leo, Sagittarius
EARTH: Taurus, Virgo, Capricorn
AIR: Gemini, Libra, Aquarius
WATER: Cancer, Scorpio, Pisces

Qualities

CARDINAL	FIXED	MUTABLE
Aries	Taurus	Gemini
Cancer	Leo	Virgo
Libra	Scorpio	Sagittarius
Capricorn	Aquarius	Pisces

CARDINAL signs mark the beginning of each new season — active.
FIXED signs represent the season at its height — steadfast.
MUTABLE signs herald a change of season — variable.

Celestial Bodies
Generating Energy of the Cosmos

Sun: birth sign, ego, identity
Moon: emotions, memories, personality
Mercury: communication, intellect, skills
Venus: love, pleasures, the fine arts
Mars: energy, challenges, sports
Jupiter: expansion, religion, happiness
Saturn: responsibility, maturity, realities
Uranus: originality, science, progress
Neptune: dreams, illusions, inspiration
Pluto: rebirth, renewal, resources

Glossary of Aspects

Conjunction: two planets within the same sign or less than 10 degrees apart, favorable or unfavorable according to the nature of the planets.

Sextile: a pleasant, harmonious aspect occurring when two planets are two signs or 60 degrees apart.

Square: a major negative effect resulting when planets are three signs from one another or 90 degrees apart.

Trine: planets four signs or 120 degrees apart, forming a positive and favorable influence.

Quincunx: planets are 150 degrees or about 5 signs apart. The hand of fate is at work and unique challenges can develop. Sometimes a karmic situation emerges.

Opposition: a six sign or 180° separation of planets generating positive or negative forces depending on the planets involved.

The Houses — *Twelve Areas of Life*

1st house: appearance, image, identity
2nd house: money, possessions, tools
3rd house: communications, siblings
4th house: family, domesticity, security
5th house: romance, creativity, children
6th house: daily routine, service, health

7th house: marriage, partnerships, union
8th house: passion, death, rebirth, soul
9th house: travel, philosophy, education
10th house: fame, achievement, mastery
11th house: goals, friends, high hopes
12th house: sacrifice, solitude, privacy

Eclipses

Elements of surprise, odd weather patterns, change and growth are linked to eclipses. Those with a birthday within three days of an eclipse can expect some shifts in the status quo. There are four eclipses this year; two are partial and two are total.

August 7, 2017 Full Moon partial lunar eclipse in Aquarius, south node

August 21, 2017 New Moon total solar eclipse in Leo, north node

January 31, 2018 Full Moon total lunar eclipse in Leo, north node

February 15, 2018 New Moon partial solar eclipse in Aquarius, south node

A total eclipse is more influential than a partial. Eclipses conjunct the Moon's north node are thought to be more favorable than those which conjoin the south node.

Retrograde Planetary Motion

Astrologically retrogrades are quite significant, promising different paths and perspectives. (Note: There is no Mars retrograde cycle this year.).

Mercury Retrograde

Impacts technology, travel and communication. Those who have been out of touch return. Revise, review and tread familiar paths. Gemini and Virgo are most affected.

April 10, 2017–May 4, 2017
in Taurus and Aries
August 13, 2017–Sept. 5, 2017
in Virgo and Leo
Dec. 3, 2017–Dec. 23, 2017
in Sagittarius

Venus Retrograde

Influences art, finances and love. Taurus and Libra are most affected.

March 4, 2017–April 15, 2017
in Aries and Pisces

Jupiter Retrograde

Large animals, speculation, education and religion are impacted. Sagittarius and Pisces are most affected.

Feb. 6, 2017–June 9, 2017
in Libra
March 9, 2018–July 10, 2018
in Scorpio

Saturn Retrograde

Elderly people, the disadvantaged, employment and natural resources are linked to Saturn. Capricorn and Aquarius are most affected.

April 6, 2017–August 25, 2017
in Sagittarius

Uranus Retrograde

Inventions, science, electronics, revolutionaries and extreme weather relate to Uranus retrograde. Aquarius is most affected.

August 3, 2017–Jan. 2, 2018 in Aries

Neptune Retrograde

Water, aquatic creatures, chemicals, spiritual forces and psychic phenomena are impacted by Neptune retrograde. Pisces is most affected.

June 16, 2017–Nov. 22, 2017
in Pisces

Pluto Retrograde

Ecology, espionage, birth and death rates, nuclear power and mysteries relate to Pluto retrograde. Scorpio is most affected.

April 20, 2017–Sept. 28, 2017
in Capricorn

ARIES
March 20–April 19
Spring 2017–Spring 2018 for those
born under the sign of the Ram

The beginning of all things is linked with this first sign of the zodiac. Primal in nature and dynamic, you tend to act spontaneously. There is a natural zest for life, with an impulse to explore and expand. An idealistic pioneer, Aries embraces all that is fresh and new. Your natural self-confidence makes an impression on others. You often shine in the role of a leader.

From the Vernal Equinox through All Fools Day, retrograde Venus is conjunct your Sun. Creative projects can be revamped. An old love is rekindled, but for good or ill the same patterns repeat in a relationship. The first three weeks of April find Mars, your ruler, highlighting the 2nd house of finances and earnings. Hard work brings rewards. Focus extra effort on using your salable job skills and security will be enhanced by your birthday. Late April–May 15 Mercury's transit in Aries favors writing, travel and study. Chant aloud on May Day to invoke a favor from Maia. Place a tulip, the flower of Aries and a symbol of perfect love, on the altar.

Late May through June 5 is especially happy and upbeat. Venus transits your sign again, making strong aspects to Saturn and Uranus. Relationships stabilize; business and pleasure combine gracefully. Pathways open to make life more comfortable and beautiful in many ways. June 6–July 20 finds Mars affecting your sector of home and family life. A house blessing at the Summer Solstice helps promote harmony. A relative might need encouragement. Seek ways to improve living arrangements. A home improvement project or a move is possible.

Throughout August, Mercury affects your health sector, which favors learning more about wellness. Rethink your dietary and exercise habits. During the last days of summer others set a positive example and offer worthwhile suggestions. The New Moon on September 20 reveals the specifics. From the Autumnal Equinox through October 10, Jupiter bids farewell to a long transit in your 7th house. You realize how an important relationship has matured and feel a sense of gratitude for the support a partnership has brought. The Full Moon in Aries on October 5 is flavored by Uranus and favors expressing original ideas. Liberty will be a priority.

All Hallows brings a competitive mood. Release energy and stress with activity. A ceremonial dance or evening stroll helps attune you to the magic of the season. Mars opposes your Sun through December 9. This powerful aspect can generate great inspiration and motivation if you rein in anger and impatience. This is especially true if you're coping with a competitive situation.

December finds Mercury, the Sun, Saturn and Venus playing tag in your 9th house. A pilgrimage to a sacred site may appeal as the Winter Solstice approaches. You would enjoy learning experiences, particularly those involving philosophy or foreign languages. An in-law or grandchild brightens holiday celebrations. By January, Saturn crosses your midheaven to begin a long transit through your career sector. The winter has a solemn quality. You might feel dedicated to high profile projects which are a challenge but also have the potential to bring great rewards.

January 19–February 10, Venus transits your 11th house. Your circle of friends widens. It's a good time to become more active within a worthwhile organization. The lunar eclipse on February 15 widens the scope of your goals. This can encourage you to discard a situation you've outgrown.

Late February–March 6, Mercury joins Neptune and Chiron in your 12th house, making you more introspective. An affinity for ecology and an attraction to remote wilderness areas may arise. A dream brings insight near the New Moon on March 17. There is a strong focus on enhancing your public image and good name as spring draws near. Keep the importance of credibility in mind and all will be well.

HEALTH
The retrograde Mercury cycle August 13–September 5 highlights your health sector and is revealing regarding a health situation. Late summer into early autumn is an ideal time to make needed changes and to examine how hereditary influences might impact health. Your intuition regarding health care facilitates wellness near the Full Moon on March 1.

LOVE
Eclipses on August 21 and January 31 affect your 5th house of love. Interesting twists, turns and revelations brighten romance then. Be receptive to growth regarding relationship issues. Jupiter exits your 7th house on October 10. A partnership will have grown and a loved one can seem more secure during the autumn and winter seasons.

SPIRITUALITY
Reflect upon Tarot Key 4, The Emperor. This commanding and self-confident image of the warrior Ares is a side of you and can awaken you from the nightmare of being controlled by outside influences. The color red, musical note C natural and the ruby (banishes grief, draws friends) will open spiritual connections through your Tarot card. December brings meaningful spiritual insights this year.

FINANCE
Spring welcomes a Mars transit which favors enthusiasm and motivation as well as some anger issues related to money. Hard work at that time will bring financial rewards. At the Winter Solstice Saturn moves into a square aspect to your Sun, an influence which prevails throughout the winter. You will long for greater success and status. Fulfill promises and responsibilities to acquire long-term security.

TAURUS
April 20–May 20
Spring 2017–Spring 2018 for those
born under the sign of the Bull

Taurus is about manifestation and putting down roots in a deeply material world. Harmonious, beautiful and comfortable surroundings are cherished by this Venus-ruled sign. After contemplating potentials, you will form a strategy. Then, when prepared, you will act, keeping in mind the goal of preserving the best interests of yourself and loved ones. Responsibility in acquiring and caring for quality possessions is always a focus.

Spring begins with Venus in retrograde motion. There can be some old projects to review before you are ready to move forward. The force of habits, both positive and negative, will be at work. After April 15 the pace picks up. On May Eve place a bouquet of iris, a flower especially linked to your sign, on the altar to attract wisdom and eloquence. A Mars conjunction to your Sun motivates you just before your birthday. The New Moon in Taurus on April 26 helps you to formulate future goals. Mid-May through early June a Mercury transit brings restlessness. Travel, multitasking and examining new information can affect the status quo. June 7–July 4, Venus conjoins your Sun while making a graceful trine to Pluto. This is wonderful for gardening, camping and other outdoor activities. Creative craft projects using clay, crystals or jewelry-making supplies can be rewarding. Make a wish related to love at the Summer Solstice, as summer's long, bright days favor romance.

The first three weeks of July find Mars sextile your Sun and creating a stir in your 3rd house. This busy and energetic trend finds you making short journeys and exchanging ideas. It's a great time to make applications and seek positions. July 22–September 5, several transits highlight your 4th house of home and family life. Decorating your dwelling, a real estate investment and genealogy can be captivating interests. At Lammastide, poignant recollections from years past surface. Consider a reunion with a childhood friend or visit an elderly relative.

September accents your 5th house. A child can be a source of pride and delight. Sports, games or a hobby might appeal, especially if the activities are shared with one you care for. In October, Jupiter moves into Scorpio, your opposing sign, where it will remain through the end of the year. Companions will present ambitious plans and ideas. Trust your instincts and all will be well. An established partnership might be entering a new phase. To honor All Hallows, mirrors would provide wonderful magical accents for costumes or to decorate a ritual area or party.

The Full Moon in Taurus on November 4 ushers in a four-week cycle during which others express a desire to include you in new interests and enthusiasms. Early December emphasizes the weather and other environmental factors. A quiet, nostalgic Winter Solstice holiday would rejuvenate you. Set out favorite keepsake decorations and photos to honor memories. December 26–January 17, Venus joins the Sun and Pluto in Capricorn, making a favorable aspect pattern in your 9th house. It's a wonderful time to enroll in a study program or to explore spiritual art and music. A broader and more expansive outlook develops.

February highlights career aspirations. Light a candle and create a charm for your workplace at Candlemas. The February 15 eclipse promises changes in your professional sphere. Consider seeking a new position. The celestial forces are propelling you forward. Late February–early March finds Venus, Mercury, the Sun and Neptune clustered in your sector of friends and goals. Trust your intuition regarding new acquaintances; it's a great time for networking. In the last weeks of winter, Jupiter turns retrograde in your 7th house. A loved one can experience a temporary setback or be facing a legal issue. Your support and loyalty would be appreciated.

HEALTH
From the Vernal Equinox until October 10, Jupiter blesses your 6th house of health. This time is wonderfully healing. Since Libra, the sign of the Scales, rules this portion of your horoscope, balance holds the key to optimum health. A wholesome balance between work, rest and exercise as well as a balanced diet established now will assure good health through the remainder of the year.

LOVE
Late June to early July, late September to mid-October and late December to mid-January are times when Venus transits in Earth signs favor romance and happiness. Try attending an outdoor concert with one you would woo. This would combine your affinity for nature and your love of music to create a promising environment for true love.

SPIRITUALITY
Tarot Key 5, The Hierophant, is your connection to spirituality. Listening to divine guidance and the development of clairaudient perception are offered by this image of a wise cleric. The color red-orange, the musical note C sharp and the topaz crystal (for inspiration) will help you attune to the spiritual values expressed by this card. Maintain a daily meditation schedule to awaken spiritual perceptions. At the Winter Solstice, Saturn joins Pluto in your 9th house, ushering in a time of genuine progress in reaching spiritual goals.

FINANCE
Brainstorming about financial goals is usually helpful. Gemini rules your 2nd house of money and values. This favors studies, publications and classes about finance. The last three weeks of July are promising. There is a bright and golden Venus transit in your money sector then.

GEMINI
May 21 – June 20
Spring 2017 – Spring 2018 for those
born under the sign of the Twins

Agility of thought, lively communication and quick wit characterize Mercury-ruled Gemini. Symbolized by the Twins, you are especially able to adapt to circumstances, almost becoming a different person as situations change. You thrive on variety and excitement but dread boredom.

Spring awakens a strong 11th house influence. You will explore options concerning goals. New types of associates are included in your social circle. By All Fools Day, selections are made which will carve your experiences throughout the springtime. Mid-April finds regret and a sense of isolation prevailing as Mercury is retrograde in your 12th house. Release old disappointments, chalking them up to experience. Try positive affirmations and visualization to help you progress. The rose, symbolizing charm and discretion, is your astrological flower. Include it in May Day rites to invoke a blessing from the May Queen. May Eve finds energetic Mars in your sign, a highly motivating trend which continues until June 4. Much can be accomplished as your birthday nears, but do control anger and impatience.

Mid-June finds Mercury racing in conjunction with your Sun, aspecting Neptune, Chiron and Saturn along the way. Double-check facts and instructions; verify plans. There's a rushed quality prevailing. Much is happening simultaneously, yet you thrive on the fast pace. At the Summer Solstice attention shifts to finances. The Sun, Mercury and Mars cluster in your 2nd house. Opportunities to add to your income are presented. Hone your salable job skills or learn a new trade to enhance your financial prospects. Shop for an item you've longed for.

July 5 – 31, Venus glides through Gemini to brighten your 1st house. You'll enchant others with your charm and pleasing demeanor. Express creative ideas as well as love during summer's warm, long days. Lammastide favors both love and money situations. Throughout August and most of September, Mercury goes back and forth in your 4th house. Family life and residence are a focus. Examine options and make final decisions about your home and living arrangements near the Autumnal Equinox.

October 1 – 22, finds Mars squaring your Sun while several other transits highlight the 5th house. Passions are strong; you may feel the need to right a wrong or confront a problem. Cultivate a creative outlet or hobby to focus energy in a productive way. At All Hallows, Venus aspects your Sun favorably, generating extra appreciation for the arts. Enjoy Celtic or other mystical music and prepare seasonal decorations, perhaps arranging Indian corn in several colors as a door or table accent.

Throughout November until December 9, your energy level will remain high, as an upbeat Mars transit sets the pace. Winter sports, yoga or competitive games can appeal. Your health and vitality are improving. On December 3, the Full Moon in Gemini is wonderful for attuning to your body's needs and internal rhythms. December 3–23 is punctuated by a retrograde Mercury cycle in your relationship sector. An old connection can be rekindled; a sense of déjà vu prevails. The past foreshadows the pattern of present events. At the Winter Solstice memories are vivid and a lost keepsake mysteriously reappears.

By January, the Sun and Venus will join Saturn in your 8th house. Invested or inherited funds, as well as tax and insurance issues, can affect your financial plans. Strategy helps resolve any monetary glitches by Candlemas. Studies and philosophical or spiritual interests are heightened in early February, when several air sign transits highlight your sector of higher thought. The solar eclipse on February 15 facilitates important insights and understanding. Mars opposes your Sun late January–March 17. Adopt a live-and-let-live approach with those who don't share your viewpoints. This is a time to steer clear of argumentative situations. Confrontations can drain your energy and end in a moot point. During winter's last days, Mercury joins Uranus to activate a sextile aspect in your 11th house. This introduces new and novel ideas as well as some intriguing and bright acquaintances.

HEALTH
Nervous energy and stress is often at the root of health issues in your life. Since Gemini is an air sign, healing breathing techniques based in yoga practices can help. Also, walking on a breezy day can be therapeutic. Jupiter enters your health sector on October 11, where it will remain for an entire year. The autumn and winter months promise improved wellness.

LOVE
The Full Moon on April 11 will join Jupiter in Libra, your 5th house of love. This stirs happiness regarding matters of the heart during the springtime. A relationship sweetens and grows during the summer and early autumn. Travel with one you love during July.

SPIRITUALITY
Tarot Key 6, The Lovers, links to your birth sign. The color orange, musical note D natural and the rose quartz crystal can help awaken its messages. Deep meditation times, reflecting upon the ancient symbols portrayed in Key 6, is when spiritual growth will unfold. The lunar eclipse on August 7 impacts you in a spiritual sense. Heed dreams and be sensitive to synchronicities during the weeks following it for spiritual guidance.

FINANCE
The Moon rules your 2nd house of finances. This underscores how emotional impulses and early family conditioning can affect financial choices. The New Moon on June 23 offers insight into making changes for the better regarding finances.

CANCER
June 21 – July 22

Spring 2017 – Spring 2018 for those
born under the sign of the Crab

The Crab, soft and vulnerable, sheltered inside its hard outer shell, represents deeply protective influences. Ruled by the Moon, you are sensitive and responsive, motivated by feelings. Loyalty, persistence, patriotism and strong opinions are traits which characterize this water sign. Your home and heritage are always cherished.

Spring brings changing dynamics regarding professional aspirations. Retrograde Venus joins the Sun and Uranus in your 10th house of fame and fortune. Diplomacy is a must in coping with complex social situations. The New Moon on March 27 reveals the specifics. April 3 – 28, Venus dips into Pisces, greeted by a conjunction with Neptune. This softens tensions and dissolves a problem. Mid to late April favors spiritual studies, creative writing and photography. Honor May Day with a bouquet of lilies on the altar. The lily, the Moonchild's flower, represents purity and persuasion.

May brings a dynamic aspect pattern. Resist the temptation to overspend or overextend. Accomplishment comes to those Cancerians who stay balanced and avoid extremes. As June begins, Mars enters Cancer where it remains until July 20. Diffuse anger with humor and tolerance if situations grow stressful near the Summer Solstice. Dedicate seasonal rites to maintaining harmony. An adventurous and courageous mood prevails as you celebrate your birthday. Motivation and enthusiasm are at a peak.

July 21 shifts emphasis to your 2nd house of values, possessions and finances, a trend which continues through mid-September. Monetary stability and making the most of income-producing opportunities are priorities. At both Lammastide and the Autumnal Equinox focus magical workings on security. Light a bright green candle on the altar for prosperity and add incense of cinnamon or frankincense. Venus moves through your money sector August 26 – September 19, opening the way for more rapid progress toward financial goals.

In October, Jupiter completes a transit through your sector of home and family. You will be aware of how family life has evolved over the past year. A childhood trauma is put to rest. Mid-October accents travel, as your 3rd house is stimulated by Mars. In preparing for All Hallows, sign up for a ghost walk or visit a nearby haunted site. Strolling through a graveyard can bring a connection with friendly spirit entities. On October 31, discuss an interesting gravestone rubbing or orb photo with like-minded friends.

November finds Mercury joining Saturn in your 6th house. The well-being of an animal companion can be foremost in your thoughts. Getting organized is important, as your daily agenda is busy. November 8–30, Venus brightens your social prospects. Issue and accept invitations; others are very responsive. In early December, Mars creates a stir in your 4th house. A family member would appreciate support and encouragement. Focus on creating a beautiful, peaceful home environment for the holiday season. At the Winter Solstice, Saturn and the Sun enter your 7th house of relationships. Partnerships of all kinds emphasize responsibility. Use care in making promises involving business or personal commitments. On the shortest of days reflect upon what others bring to your life.

On January 1, the Full Moon in Cancer brings an emotional release. There is much excitement about the possibilities promised by the New Year. Charge crystals or a dreamcatcher and write a list of resolutions as the Moon rises. Venus transits your 7th house through January 17. Happiness comes through the success enjoyed by those closest to you. A conflict is resolved. Late January through early February the hand of fate is at work. Several transits will quincunx your Sun creating an odd, unbalanced sequence of events. Be observant and flexible. Consult the Tarot or runes at Candlemas for deeper insight. February 18–March 6 Mercury, Venus and Neptune join the Sun in Pisces. Your intuition guides you past a dilemma. This influence also promotes creative expression through writing or art.

During the last weeks of winter you will be highly visible as several transits activate your midheaven. Surprise opportunities arise related to professional advancement.

HEALTH

Saturn affects your 6th house of health through mid-December. Make a conscientious effort to take care of your health and fitness goals will be achievable by the Winter Solstice. Be aware especially of your teeth. Invest in good dental care. It will enhance your overall wellness now.

LOVE

August finds Venus dancing through your sign and there's an upbeat, whirlwind quality to romance then. On October 11, Jupiter begins a year-long passage through your 5th house of love. Relationship prospects improve. A cherished bond grows and matures throughout the autumn and winter months.

SPIRITUALITY

Tarot Key 7, The Chariot, is tied to your birth sign. This triumphant figure carried by a pair of sphinxes will help you journey toward higher spiritual consciousness. The times of day suggested for reflecting on this card are 3:00 AM and PM. The color orange-yellow, musical note D sharp and the kunzite stone (for stress release) can help stimulate spirituality. The emotional impact of your environment is a factor affecting spiritual growth.

FINANCE

All four of the eclipses this year profoundly affect your 2nd and 8th houses, the sectors of earned income and invested or inherited funds. Expect some changes in your finances. Avoid risks. Seek bargains. If those around you are in need, offer advice and encouragement instead of financial resources.

LEO
July 23–August 22
Spring 2017–Spring 2018 for those
born under the sign of the Lion

Radiant and warm, ruled by the Sun, Leo is regal and ambitious. With a dislike of meanness or pettiness, you have an affinity for the young and young at heart. A natural leader, the dignified Lion commands respect and deference. Self confident and generous, you strive to enjoy life, often combining business with pleasure.

Spring awakens with Mercury and Uranus igniting a spark in your 9th house. You are inspired by new concepts and possibilities. An adventurous mood prevails through May 15. Honor May Day with an arrangement of sunflowers, your astrological flower. It represents following the spiritual light. From mid-May through June 4, the influence of Mars in your 11th house accents your social circle and generates refreshing new goals. Helpful, supportive people offer encouragement near the New Moon on May 25. Mid-June finds Jupiter stationary in your 3rd house, making communication with a neighbor or sibling a bit awkward. Time heals any misunderstandings. By the Summer Solstice it will be easier to gather information and make choices. Consider enrolling in a continuing education program.

July 6–25, Mercury transits Leo. Travel, problem solving and exchanging information are all favored. Meetings during this time can be exceptionally productive. August brings two eclipses, one in Aquarius, your opposing sign and the other in Leo, conjunct your Sun. Attachments and relationships are in a state of transformation. Unexpected events are pending, perhaps an upcoming move or job change. Your birthday will be especially memorable this year.

Venus brightens your sign August 26–September 19. Finances improve. It's a good time for building relationships or expressing creative ideas. At the Autumnal Equinox, charm a loved one with a poem or greeting card and burn a deep rose-colored taper ringed by colorful foliage. October begins with Mars and Mercury transiting your 2nd house of finances. This motivates you to pursue new sources of income. Your patient and thoughtful efforts will be rewarded by All Hallows. Be a good listener while celebrating Halloween. You will encounter those who want to discuss their interesting experiences.

November finds Jupiter, the Sun, Mercury and Venus activating your 4th house. A real estate transaction, home repair or decorating project can need attention. The New Moon on November 18 highlights the specifics. Family members share thoughts regarding the future as November ends. December begins with Mercury turning retrograde in your 5th house. The winter holiday season evokes sentiment and memories. This can involve contact with someone you knew long ago. December's short, dark days favor past life regression and meditation. The Winter Solstice is beneficial for a healing ritual. Include pine and sage aromatherapy to enhance strength and wellness.

During January, Venus enters your health sector. The New Year begins with improved vitality and well-being, especially near the New Moon on January 16. The Full Moon in Leo on January 31 is a total lunar eclipse. Old patterns are breaking; you may experience a sense of reinventing yourself. At Candlemas, dedicate candles to dispel confusion.

Early February accents your 7th house of relationships. Others voice thoughts and plans which impact you. Cooperate and examine opposing viewpoints. The solar eclipse on February 15 offers more perspective on this. A partner is unpredictable. The last half of February finds planetary transits gathering in Pisces, your 8th house of mysteries and resources. It's a good time to attend a séance or consult the Ouija board. At the Full Moon on March 1 new long-term financial strategies are worth considering. An inheritance or insurance settlement could come your way. As winter wanes, strong influences affect your sector of travel and foreign places. You can be curious about global situations. March 7–20 favors making reservations and selections regarding travel or the purchase of imported items.

HEALTH
Saturn joins Pluto in Capricorn, your health sector, on the eve of the Winter Solstice. This trend lasts through the next couple of years and emphasizes the consequences of long-time health habits and the impact your work environment has on your health. Begin to make changes for the better during the spring and summer months regarding diet and other lifestyle choices.

LOVE
The Aquarius eclipses on August 7 and February 15 promise some excitement regarding relationships. Respect the wishes of a partner and all will be well. Summer ends with a Venus transit through Leo, promising a happy romantic interlude.

SPIRITUALITY
Strength, Key 8, is the Tarot card associated with Leo. It portrays a lovely lady taming a ferocious lion with patience and love. The spiritual message involves the higher self overcoming lower desires. Connect with it whenever you seek to release a burden. The color bright yellow, musical note E natural and the diamond, the gem of truth and honor, relate to your card. March–December Saturn passes through your 5th house, bringing a spiritual message concerning the rewards and challenges of caring for the needs of a loved one.

FINANCE
The spring and early summer months favor analyzing finances and making choices. Outline a long-term financial plan then. Resist the temptation to overextend and overspend after mid-October, when Jupiter moves into a challenging square aspect to your Sun.

VIRGO
August 23–September 22
Spring 2017–Spring 2018 for those
born under the sign of the Virgin

The systematic analyst of the zodiac, Virgo is on a quest to create order from a chaotic universe. Service-oriented and selective, you are discriminating and helpful while promoting structure and grounding. Ruled by Mercury, you are thoughtful and intellectual with a flair for problem solving.

The Vernal Equinox ushers in a renewed zest for life with a favorable influence from Mars in Taurus. This inspiring pattern continues through April 21. Leadership skills are present and you'll enjoy travel and sports. May Day finds Mercury retrograde, creating a nostalgic mood. Prepare seasonal decorations featuring your astrological flower, the morning glory. It symbolizes persistence and creativity. Mid-May through mid-June emphasizes competitive situations related to career aspirations with dynamic planetary transits in Gemini impacting your 10th house. A touch of humor and tolerance helps you make the best of complex situations. The Full Moon on June 9 conjoins Saturn in your 4th house. A family or household situation needs attention.

The Summer Solstice glows with love and harmony. A Venus-Pluto trine favorably influences you from late June through July 4. The rest of July brings an 11th house emphasis, pointing to politics or community concerns. Consider becoming more involved in an organization. By Lammastide, Mercury will be in Virgo, where it will remain throughout August. You will be juggling a variety of different projects. A transportation need can be involved in this. Mars enters your 1st house as September begins, favoring enthusiasm and a competitive spirit. This high energy trend prevails through October 22. Much is accomplished. The New Moon in Virgo on September 20 accents the importance of your image and making a good impression. At the Autumnal Equinox take time to understand and "know thyself," as the ancient oracle said. You are creating your reality in a very big way now.

The first half of October brings a Venus conjunction to your Sun. Social prospects are promising, as is shopping for needed items and seeking additional income, through October 14. By All Hallows, Mercury, Jupiter and the Sun are in your 3rd house and sextile your Sun. You will delight in puzzles, poems, stories and jokes with a Halloween theme. November 6 begins a Mercury transit through your 4th house. It's punctuated by a retrograde cycle. Secrets about relatives, domestic situations and household decorating and repairs are all important concerns during the holiday season. Holiday plans can be uncertain. Be flexible December 3–23, while Mercury is retrograde. At the Winter Solstice focus on release and forgiveness. Donate items which no longer serve you to charity.

Late December through January 17 finds Venus joining Pluto and the Sun in your 5th house of pleasure and romance. Share a favorite pastime with one you admire. The expression of creative ideas enriches your life in a serendipitous way. The New Moon in Capricorn on January 16 heals an old heartache. The last days of January are highlighted by a favorable Mercury aspect. A business trip is productive. Information shared by an acquaintance offers fresh and useful perspectives.

Wild creatures and companion animals assume greater importance during February as your 6th and 12th houses are activated. You could find involvement in a pet rescue or wildlife rehabilitation rewarding. On March 1 the Full Moon in Virgo heightens your charm and charisma. Others notice and admire you. Expect to be the center of attention; there might even be some public recognition early in the month. As winter fades into spring, Jupiter turns retrograde in your 3rd house. A recurring situation involving a neighbor or sibling needs attention. Clear communication holds the key to smoothing over any differences. Positive affirmations and visualization can be very effective.

HEALTH

The eclipse on August 7 affects your health sector and can bring some changes regarding wellness factors. Health care professionals can offer new suggestions. Throughout the year adjustments to what has been status quo regarding health care choices can be helpful.

LOVE

Pluto hovers in the middle of your 5th house of love all year. Explore the possibility of soul mate or past life connections with one who is dear to you. The Full Moon on July 9 is conjunct Pluto, providing a catalyst for deep spiritual connections to surface. True love is going through a transformation. Venus and Mars dance hand-in-hand in Virgo during September and October. The late summer and early autumn show promise regarding love connections.

SPIRITUALITY

Your Tarot card, Key 9, The Hermit, presents valuable spiritual insights. Walking alone, hinting at a solitary vision quest, this wise teacher holds a light for others to follow. The color lime green, musical note F natural and the sapphire (for protection and peace) will aid in following the guidance offered. The quiet predawn hours are a favorable time to meditate upon The Hermit. The eclipses on August 21 and January 31 fall in your 12th house. Spiritual revelations are likely near those dates.

FINANCE

From the Vernal Equinox through April 15 Venus, ruler of your 2nd house of finance, will be retrograde. Avoid any risks regarding financial issues then. In late December, Saturn changes signs, moving out of a square aspect to your Sun. Old debts or other financial obligations lessen, allowing you to move forward in reaching financial goals during the winter.

LIBRA
September 23–October 23
Spring 2017–Spring 2018 for those
born under the sign of the Scales

Meaningful interaction with others characterizes sociable Libra. Symbolized by the Scales, you seek balance and respect justice. Weighing alternatives, you arrive at a well considered opinion when a decision must be made. Ruled by gracious Venus, you express charm and gentle good humor while surrounding yourself with beauty.

Spring begins with a pervasive note of reflection and remembrance with Venus retrograde until April 15. Others have opposing tastes and priorities. Compromise and tolerance will smooth over differences. Gather pansies to decorate for your May Eve celebrations. The pansy symbolizes thoughtfulness. It has a traditional affinity with your sign. By May Day, Mars transits Gemini and your 9th house. Travel and adventure will beckon; your vitality and enthusiasm will be high. Much is accomplished throughout May and early June. The second and third weeks of June bring a favorable Mercury aspect assuring easy, clever expression of ideas. A controversial issue can be successfully addressed by the Summer Solstice. Include peace symbols on your altar to honor the longest of days.

During July, the emphasis shifts to financial security and money management. Since Mars and the Sun are involved, it's important to simply enjoy what you have while controlling any anger or stress related to material desires. By Lammas, a Jupiter-Pluto square accents awareness of how the world situation impacts you personally. Analyze how shifting economic trends and social issues can best be adapted to your own priorities. August generates tremendous growth. The eclipse on August 21 clarifies goals and attracts associates that are catalysts for advancement.

During September, Mercury and Mars will join the Sun in your 12th house. Summer's last days find you introspective and reserved, cherishing some quiet time. A dream conveys important messages near the New Moon on September 20. Dedicate spiritual observances to blessing charitable endeavors at the Autumnal Equinox. Mercury transits Libra through the first half of October. Worthwhile travel opportunities arise near your birthday. This might include a visit to a unique bookstore or library.

Late October is brightened by a lovely Venus conjunction to your Sun, which remains until November 7. Accept invitations at All Hallows and purchase new finery and art objects. It's time to beautify yourself and your surroundings. By early November, a dynamic Mars transit in Libra will be agitating things. This highly motivating energy carries you through December 9. Much can be accomplished if you keep anger and impatience in check. Exercise offers the best release from stress. Retrograde Mercury affects your 3rd house throughout most of December. Concentrate. Holiday plans are in flux; it's important to communicate and verify plans with others. Allow extra time if traveling. Items which seem to disappear can return mysteriously just after the Winter Solstice. Humor, absurdity and misrule are perfect themes to keep in mind while celebrating deep winter.

During January, Saturn and the Sun are joined by Venus and Mercury in your 4th house of home and family. Making your residence more comfortable and beautiful is a priority. This might involve purchasing a new home. Responsibilities linked to family obligations are accented. By Candlemas the mood lightens. A creative project or romantic interlude is planned in early February. Valentine's Day is especially memorable.

The last half of February through early March shifts priorities toward maintaining good health. Meditation and visualization build a positive mind-body connection. A beloved animal companion can facilitate improved health and emotional well-being near the New Moon on March 17. As winter ends, Jupiter turns retrograde in your 2nd house of cash flow. Live within your means and all will be well regarding finances.

HEALTH
On April 11 the Full Moon in Libra conjoins Jupiter, the celestial healer, in your 1st house. This shows progress in reaching health goals and an awareness of what your body needs to stay in optimum condition. Jupiter remains in Libra until October 10. This entire six-month period is very promising for healing and attaining fitness goals.

LOVE
There will be two eclipses this year in your 5th house of love, one on August 7 and another on February 15. Expect some sparkle and surprises. Allow intimate relationships to evolve and grow near those dates. July 5–31 and October 15–November 7 bring wonderful Venus transits which usher in whispers of true love.

SPIRITUALITY
Justice, Tarot Key 11, is associated with Libra. Meditate on it to deepen spirituality. Balance, examining options, fairness and receiving what is deserved are Justice's message. The color green, the musical note F sharp and the carnelian agate (for good cheer) are linked to your card and can be incorporated into spiritual workings. Visit scenic outdoor settings to help restore equilibrium and enable spiritual growth. Late September, just before your birthday, especially favors spiritual awakening.

FINANCE
Jupiter, the planet of luck and opportunity, will enter your financial sector in mid-October where it will remain for about a year. This brightens the financial picture from your birthday on. Just avoid overextending with high risk ventures. Advice offered by others should be considered carefully. Uranus is oppose your Sun all year and this can attract intriguing associates who don't use the most sound financial judgment.

SCORPIO

October 24–November 21

Spring 2017–Spring 2018 for those
born under the sign of the Scorpion

Intense and purposeful, Scorpio is about cycles of transformation and renewal. You seek ever deeper insight into meaningful matters. Intimately connected to the world of the subconscious, this Mars and Pluto-ruled sign is never superficial. You are able to appreciate life's ironies and coincidences with subtle humor.

The Vernal Equinox brings a twinge of spring fever. You'll feel pensive and ready for something fresh and novel because Venus, Uranus and Mercury join the Sun in your health sector. After All Fools' Day, the ideas of others offer a shift in perspective. April accents the value of cooperation and supporting others. By May, Mars is in your 8th house. Long-range financial planning, perhaps involving taxes, insurance or an investment, will be a focus. The orchid, representative of beauty and refinement, is your flower. Include it on your altar during May Eve ceremonies to attract positive energies.

The Full Moon in Scorpio on May 10 ushers in a four-week cycle when you will want to right wrongs and share knowledge. You can inspire others during late May and early June. June 8–July 4, Venus transits your 7th house. This favors any legal issues you have pending; it's also supportive of relationships. You will bask in the joyful accomplishments of someone who is near and dear. At the Summer Solstice group chants or affirmations can empower a sense of camaraderie. A Venus quincunx to your Sun colors the last three weeks of July. Fate plays a role in relationship issues. A past life or karmic connection is likely. Research can change your plans regarding either love or money. At Lammas, give thanks for the insights you've gained.

August brings eclipses in your 4th and 10th houses. You'll be juggling work and family obligations. Be receptive to changes regarding residence or your career path near August 7 and 21. September 1–6 retrograde Mercury brings a hectic and competitive note regarding career aspirations. Be patient and look at all options. Near the Autumnal Equinox your 12th house is highlighted. Time spent in deep reverie and meditation brings perspective and generates confidence. Pluto completes a long retrograde cycle and turns direct as September ends. Old doors are closing. Forgive, forget and release.

The first half of October accents your 11th house. You can feel drawn into community life and service organizations. Jupiter enters Scorpio in mid-October for a year-long stay. Your world widens, promising tremendous growth. At All Hallows, reflect upon developing potentials. As November begins, Mercury is strong. Pursue travel opportunities near your birthday. November 8–30, Venus conjoins your Sun, generating a very sociable mood. Others will be attracted to you. Cultivate new friendships and follow through with artistic or musical ventures.

December accents past financial patterns. Avoid repeating what hasn't worked before, as retrograde Mercury affects your 2nd house of cash flow. December 10–January 26, Mars races through Scorpio. You'll feel especially motivated and energetic, but keep a handle on anger. At the Winter Solstice add greenery to your altar to invoke prosperity. December 23–January 11 brings a favorable Mercury-Uranus aspect involving your 2nd and 6th houses. Business-related travel and thoughts shared by concerned associates are helpful. The last part of January finds several transits in Capricorn involving your 3rd house. You will be very busy and multitasking. Transportation arrangements are successfully resolved. This might involve the purchase of a new vehicle.

Candlemas restores peace and harmony at home, as Venus and the Sun glide through your 4th house of residence and family. Situations regarding your housing will be positive through mid-February. The eclipse on February 15 brings a surprise regarding your heritage. The end of February through March 20 finds several Pisces transits tagging Neptune in your sector of pleasure and romance. A new avocation or artistic venture brightens the last days of winter. Happiness is shared with one you love very much.

HEALTH
Uranus affects your health sector all year, generating an abundance of nervous energy. Pace exercise sessions gradually; don't overdo it with really strenuous activity all at once. Health improves just before your birthday when Jupiter enters Scorpio.

LOVE
Dreamy and elusive Neptune impacts your 5th house of love all year. A seaside getaway or cruise sets the scene for idyllic love liaisons. The Full Moon on September 6 ushers in a promising cycle for love. November and March favor tender interludes also.

SPIRITUALITY
Tarot Key 20, Judgment, is linked with your co-ruler Pluto and offers spiritual insights. It shows the angel Gabriel sounding a trumpet call to a new life. Incorporate the color red, musical note C natural and petrified wood, an emblem of eternity, into your spiritual work. Contemplate the day's activities and your mission in life in the evening, just before going to sleep. Pluto's retrograde cycle in your 3rd house April 17–September 28, 2017 favors spiritual studies and discussions.

FINANCE
Sober, serious Saturn has transited your 2nd house of finances during the past several years, creating responsibilities and restrictions. This ends at the Winter Solstice. Stick to your budget and work patiently early in the year. A better phase regarding finances can be expected by January. Lucky Jupiter enters Scorpio in October, bringing a bright glimmer of the good fortune to come.

SAGITTARIUS
November 22–December 21
Spring 2017–Spring 2018 for those
born under the sign of the Archer

Sincere, extroverted and gifted with uncanny insight, this Jupiter-ruled fire sign is outspoken and forward thinking. You are especially connected to animals, as your symbol the Centaur suggests. Targeting the truth with an arrow poised to shoot, your emblem also reveals a certain bluntness coupled with a competitive nature. You approach life as a game to be played and won.

The Vernal Equinox is welcomed by Jupiter retrograde. Goals and desires are fluctuating. Associates are unpredictable; they might express ideas which differ from yours. On April 29, Venus enters your 5th house of love where it will remain until early June. The springtime promises romantic bliss. Accept and issue invitations near May Day. The jasmine, which represents cherished friendships, is your flower. Include it in seasonal garlands and other decorations. On June 9 the Full Moon is in your sign, accenting teamwork. You'll appreciate a supportive partnership. At the Summer Solstice Mars and the Sun highlight your 8th house, an influence which prevails through July 20. The afterlife and reincarnation captivate you. Summer sunsets offer glimpses into other dimensions. Heed a message brought by a spectral visitor or the fey folk.

Just before Lammas, Mars enters your sister fire sign of Leo where it brightens your sector of higher education and faraway places. An educational journey, perhaps involving a safari or eco-adventure travel, is appealing. Expect an abrupt shift after August 26 when Saturn changes direction in your sign. Important work and concerns come to your attention. Others depend upon you throughout the late summer and autumn months. September accents your career sector. Your visibility comes to the fore. Put your best foot forward and strive to make the best possible impression as the Autumnal Equinox draws near. You'll have an opportunity to demonstrate your highest potentials. This can lead to a promotion or other significant offer in the future.

September ends with several transits opposing Neptune, generating confusion regarding family situations or real estate transactions. Make a special effort to communicate with relatives. A house blessing would be beneficial. Use sandalwood incense and ring a bell to invoke a calming, helpful ambience around your dwelling. Jupiter enters your 12th house in mid-October. This has been called the "guardian angel" influence. Support comes to you from behind the scenes. Dreams and quiet contemplation offer valuable insights near All Hallows.

Early November finds Mercury beginning a long passage through your sign, a trend lasting through January 10. It's a wonderful time to complete a course of study or write that book you've been talking about. The New Moon in Sagittarius on December 18 helps you focus and refine details. At the Winter Solstice others express enthusiasm for your suggestions. Have a brainstorming session over cups of hot mulled cider on the longest of nights. Saturn moves out of Sagittarius as December ends. A sense of ease prevails. By New Year's Eve you'll feel very upbeat. Early to mid-January finds Venus joining the Sun in your 2nd house of finances. Express creative ideas about business. Artistry adds to your income. Friends might suggest lucrative work or offer recommendations which help you financially. The eclipse on January 31 shifts your focus to philosophical and spiritual concerns. Select blue tapers, symbolizing peace and protection, to honor Candlemas.

In early February your sector of travel and communication is accented. The pace of daily life is rapid. Heed conversations and newscasts. It's worthwhile to keep up with current events both in your own social circle and the world at large throughout February. During March an energetic Mars conjunction to your Sun encourages motivation and accomplishment. Quell anger and impatience as winter wanes and all will be well.

HEALTH

During the past several years Saturn, which impacts health, has been in your sign. Past health habits and your heredity have impacted wellness. During the spring and summer take care of your body with enough rest, light exercise and natural foods. When Saturn changes signs just after your birthday your vitality should improve.

LOVE

Unpredictable Uranus is retrograde August 3–January 2 in your 5th house of love. An old flame might be rekindled. There can be changes in your preferences regarding love. December 1–25 finds Venus, the cosmic love goddess, in your 1st house. The winter holiday season is warmed by true love. An admirer plans a birthday surprise.

SPIRITUALITY

Your Tarot card is Key 14, Temperance. Its unique spiritual images include Michael, the archangel of fire, combining an alchemical healing concoction beneath a sunlit sky. Bright royal blue, the musical note G sharp and the amethyst crystal, symbolizing truth and spirituality, are associated with Key 14 and can be useful in your spiritual practices. Attune to spiritual energies outdoors during the late morning, just before noon. Two eclipses, on August 7 and January 31, affect your 9th house of higher thought. New spiritual realizations are likely near those dates.

FINANCE

During August your 8th house of invested and inherited funds is brightened by Venus. Some extra money or property can come your way then. During the winter Saturn begins a long passage through your 2nd house of earnings. Learning new salable skills and patient effort will lead to financial advantages in the long-term future. January will bring the specifics into focus.

CAPRICORN

December 22–January 19

Spring 2017–Spring 2018 for those
born under the sign of the Goat

Symbolized by the rugged Goat and the element earth, this Saturn-ruled sign meets challenging situations with practical perseverance. Capable and responsible, you have a fatalistic way of making the best of life situations. Ambitious Capricorn ventures forever onward and upward, focused on reaching new heights.

As the springtime dawns, Mars makes a favorable trine aspect to your Sun. Your energy and enthusiasm are at a peak. A new hobby, social connections or creative projects captivate you through April 21. By May Eve, retrograde Mercury impacts your home and family life. The carnation, representing success and energy, is your flower. Place a bouquet on a table or altar to bless your residence while honoring the holiday. Consider redecorating or making household re-pairs. From mid-May through early June, transits in Taurus encourage travel and exchanging information. Listen carefully. Worthwhile information comes your way during casual conversations.

A promising influence from Venus brightens your life from June 7 to early July. Enjoy a concert, art gallery or other cultural event. Plan a garden party or outdoor picnic to honor the Summer Solstice. Someone you love and admire will be favorably impressed. Younger people are a source of pride and inspiration as summer begins. The Full Moon on July 9 in your sign ushers in a busy time. Several cardinal sign aspects pull you in different directions. You are at the center of attention and assume a position of leadership. By Lammas, Venus enters your 7th house. A talented and thoughtful partner offers support.

Life is less demanding during August. The eclipse on August 21 emphasizes your 8th house. During the following days omens point to messages from the spirit world. Mysteries are resolved; a lost item might be found unexpectedly. As the Autumnal Equinox nears you'll be attracted to faraway places. Overseas travel for a spiritual pilgrimage, study or business can be appealing during September.

October 1–10 the Sun and Mercury will cluster with Jupiter at your midheaven. A promotion, new career opportunity or other professional recognition is likely. The momentum continues as All Hallows nears. You will feel compelled to achieve more and move forward.

November brings benevolent transits in your 11th house. The mood is altruistic. Friendships are a blessing. Involvement in community life or organizations brings rewards. The New Moon on November 18 reveals the specifics. December finds you rethinking commitments and alliances. Retrograde Mercury in your sector of solitude and privacy tends to make you more introspective. At the Winter

Solstice listen to the small, still voice within as you meditate by candlelight. A charm or picture featuring a snowflake design reminds you to cherish your individuality. As your birthday approaches you'll embrace nonconformity.

December 26–January 17, Venus brightens your 1st house. Your charisma level and charm are at a peak. Both business and personal situations are promising; you will find much to feel grateful for. Your sector of finances is highlighted as January ends. Be aware of how changes in your profession can involve updating job skills. The eclipses on January 31 and February 15 can usher in changes to the status quo regarding your source of income. Research new earning and investment opportunities during February.

Early March emphasizes communication and information exchange. A neighbor or sibling reaches out to you. The end of the winter is dynamic. Mars enters your sign on March 18, bringing a burst of energy and initiative.

HEATH

Your 6th house of health is ruled by Mercury. Staying informed about wellness topics is important. Find health care professionals who are willing to offer guidance and suggestions. April 22–June 4 is a good time to select health goals and consider new regimes. Saturn enters Capricorn on December 20 where it will stay for the next couple of years. Lifestyle choices made then will determine your health for the long-term future. Focus on caring for your teeth and skin during the winter months.

LOVE

Beautiful outdoor scenery, especially if there are mountains, provides a perfect backdrop for pursuing true love. Venus and the element earth rule your 5th house of love. Sincerity, a love of music, and stability are qualities which you would seek in a romantic partner. June, January and the week of the Full Moon on November 4 are times when the celestial patterns favor love.

SPIRITUALITY

The World, Tarot Key 21, linked with Saturn, offers you meaningful spiritual guidance. This card portrays a dancer, supporting herself on air through her own efforts. She is surrounded by a wreath which represents cycles and attainment. The message is that the freedom to move in any direction is the reward of continuous effort. Reflect upon this card whenever you feel overwhelmed. The color blue-violet, musical note A and the garnet (a crystal symbolizing virtue and friendship) can assist in spiritual work. The Winter Solstice this year comes just as Saturn enters your sign. Meaningful ceremonies celebrating winter can deepen your spirituality.

FINANCE

Your money sector is influenced by Uranus. New trends and technology related to finance will always appeal to you. From the Vernal Equinox through October 9 a fortunate Jupiter transit blesses your 10th house of status and recognition. Progress you're able to make in attaining professional goals from the springtime through the early autumn promises improved finances.

AQUARIUS

January 20–February 18
Spring 2017–Spring 2018 for those
born under the sign of the Water Bearer

The idealistic and open-minded Water
Bearer pouring from a jar generously
offers refreshing truth. Ruled by free-
dom-loving Uranus you are accepting
of all points of view and lifestyles. This
detached and paradoxical air sign projects
a cool objectivity while curiously examining all that is odd or innovative.

The Vernal Equinox arrives with an
exchange of ideas prompted by the Sun,
Mercury and Uranus in your 3rd house.
This brings a brainstorming session which
continues until All Fools Day. It generates
new perspectives. Venus hovers in your
money sector April 3–28. Bargains can
be found. A friend's assistance can be a
key factor in generating a windfall. By
May Eve, passionate Mars affects your
love and pleasure sector. This enthusiasm
remains through June 4, bringing fun and
excitement. To celebrate and honor May
Day, include snowdrops and other tiny
white flowers, which represent hope, on
your altar.

During the 2nd and 3rd weeks of June,
Mercury dashes through Gemini while
making a favorable aspect to your Sun.
Plan vacation activities. Initiate conversations. Romance is promising. At
the Summer Solstice bless a cherished
relationship with loving affirmations.
Offer an exchange of small, meaningful
tokens. July begins with Mars emphasizing your health sector. Wear a hat and
sunscreen when outdoors in the summer
heat. Observe how anger or stress can
impact your well-being. Mild exercise
can help restore balance and provide a
wholesome release of aggravation. By
Lammastide, several transits involving fire signs emphasize social connections, teamwork and the news media.
Transformations are evolving around
you. The lunar eclipse in Aquarius on
August 7 underscores this. Be flexible
and observant through the remainder
of the month. Questions of loyalty and
legality can arise. After September 5 the
confusion should dissipate.

During September your thoughts dwell
upon mysteries and afterlife communication. Dreams and omens offer valuable
guidance. The hand of fate is at work
with Mars, the Sun and Mercury forming a quincunx aspect involving your 8th
house. The Autumnal Equinox ushers in a
refreshing shift. The seasonal colors and
cooler weather bring a sense of release.
The shadowy undercurrents of tension
which were present during the late summer fade. You're ready to move forward.

October offers widening horizons.
Mercury and Venus in Libra will trine
your Sun, highlighting your 9th house
of higher consciousness. Foreign languages and imported items intrigue
you. At All Hallows, glimpses of the
historical traditions surrounding the
holiday offer spiritual solace. November

finds Jupiter highlighting your sector of fame and status where it will remain for nearly a year. Near the New Moon on November 18 seek a promotion and make the most of your visibility. You'll find yourself at the center of attention as December begins. Just before the Winter Solstice Saturn exits your sector of friendships and goals, where it has created some false starts in the recent past. You'll be able to extricate yourself from persons or situations that have been draining your energy and resources. On December 21 focus on what you would like to release. Reclaim your freedom in the peaceful darkness of the year's longest night.

As January begins you will be in the mood for quiet contemplation. A 12th house influence sets the pace, emphasizing reverie and privacy. You can feel connected with the natural world and wild creatures during the weeks before your birthday. The eclipse in Leo on January 31 brings a surprise announcement involving a partner or team member. At Candlemas bless a votive candle for resolving opposing viewpoints. The first part of February, as the eclipse in Aquarius on February 15 approaches, is an interesting time. Prepare for adjustments and growth. February 16–28 accents Neptune in your 2nd house of finances. Follow hunches regarding money management. An inspiration or creative idea can generate extra income.

March promises variety and a fast pace. Transits in your 3rd house emphasize multitasking and new ideas. Organization is essential in order to keep up with many projects requiring attention, at home and at work alike.

HEALTH
Retrograde Uranus in your 3rd house, August 3–January 2, indicates that examining health and safety factors in your neighborhood can help in making wise choices which will bolster your wellness. Seek efficiency and comfort regarding transportation to promote a more relaxed lifestyle, encouraging improved health.

LOVE
The year ahead brings two eclipses in your 7th house of relationships. Partnerships are evolving; your nearest and dearest can surprise you. Approach love as an adventure and all will be well. Venus aspects augur a summer of love.

SPIRITUALITY
Your Tarot card is Key 17, The Star. The image is of a lovely lady water bearer generously pouring unconditional love. The color purple, musical note A sharp and the moldavite crystal (symbolizing wisdom from outer space) can be useful in spiritual workings with this card. Early winter highlights your 12th house. This favors solitary meditation while seeking spiritual truths from within.

FINANCE
A fortunate Jupiter transit through Libra, your sister air sign, promises financial gain between the early spring and mid-October. Be careful not to be overly generous with friends in need though. Saturn's influence indicates that people nearby could drain your resources. Offer advice and encouragement, but protect your own financial interests.

PISCES
February 19–March 20
Spring 2017–Spring 2018 for those
born under the sign of the Fish

Sensitive and adaptable Pisces is symbolized by two Fish, joined together yet swimming in different directions. Ruled by dreamy, elusive Neptune, you are a study in contradictions. Pisceans are kind and caring, yet will often become the catalyst which dissolves established situations, upsetting the status quo to make way for new growth.

Budgeting and accepting financial parameters are important at the Vernal Equinox. Venus is retrograde in your money sector; this might tempt you to overextend or overspend. April 2–21, Mercury and Mars make positive aspects to your Sun. This generates solutions to complex situations. Helpful information arrives. Examine past patterns. They reveal what to expect for the future. All types of violets, representative of reserve and dignity, are your flowers. Include them in bouquets to honor the holiday. By May Day, a Mars transit accents your home and family sector. Home improvements, real estate and the needs of relatives will remain a priority through early June.

A heavy emphasis on intense mutable sign aspects in mid-June ushers in a hectic cycle. You will be juggling a variety of activities. Concentrate in order to follow through with projects and promises. At the Summer Solstice your 5th house of love and pleasure is brightened by the Sun and other transits, including Mars, in your sister water sign of Cancer. Place seashells on your altar to welcome summer and honor the holiday. The New Moon in Cancer on June 23 brings emotional fulfillment and peace. July 1–20 promises vacation opportunities. You would especially enjoy relaxing near the waterfront. Late July–August 31 brings a long Mercury transit through Virgo, your opposing sign. Companions are charming, yet there is an element of illusion afoot. Consider second opinions and look beneath the surface. All may not be as it first appears.

Your vitality improves September 1–19. Venus is well aspected in your health sector. The Full Moon in Pisces on September 6 enhances your confidence and brings an opportunity for creative expression. It's a great time to enjoy dance. At the Autumnal Equinox the Sun joins Jupiter, favoring your 8th house. A return on an investment or other financial windfall is likely to come your way by All Hallows. Others share confidences near the holiday. It is wise to remain discreet.

November 6 begins a focus in your career sector involving transits of Mercury and Saturn. Learn all you can regarding your profession. Dedication and effort will be recognized. On December 10, Mars begins a favorable aspect pattern which enhances your energy level. Your motivation will be high throughout the rest of December and most of January. Your 9th house is impacted, favoring travel, philosophical studies and writing. At the Winter Solstice your sector of friendship and humanitarian values is highlighted. As the winter holiday season peaks, charitable endeavors and selecting rewarding long-term goals will be of concern. The Full Moon on January 1 is very favorable for celebrating with those you love.

The first half of January finds Venus gliding through your 11th house along with the Sun and Saturn. Your circle of acquaintances widens. Network. You will find that others respect your advice and follow your example. The New Moon on January 16 brings the specifics into focus. As January ends, memories involving an old regret or a disappointment are heightened by planets in your 12th house. At Candlemas light three candles representing the past, present and future. Reflect on releasing the past and moving onward through the present and toward the future. Mid-February through mid-March ushers in a dynamic Mars influence. A potent competitive spirit is brewing around your professional sphere. As your birthday approaches focus on doing the best you can, then trust fate to bring the best outcome your way. The Pisces New Moon on March 17 welcomes a positive new cycle of self acceptance and appreciation. Your outlook is practical and steady as winter ends.

HEALTH
The Leo eclipses on August 21 and January 31 accent your health sector. Temperature extremes and other environmental factors can have an impact on your well-being near those times. This year favors keeping an especially positive mind-body connection. Maintaining a cheerful attitude genuinely benefits your overall health.

LOVE
Your 5th house of love is ruled by the Moon. Closely follow the Moon Calendar for insight into how the lunar phases correlate with love situations. June–July finds a fiery and passionate Mars transit influencing your love sector. An important involvement reaches a turning point at that time.

SPIRITUALITY
Tarot Key 18, The Moon, is associated with Pisces. The color magenta, musical note B and the moonstone (for emotional fulfillment) can assist spiritual practices when implemented with this card. Good times to focus on your Tarot card are in the evening while drifting into sleep and again upon awakening. The Full Moon on May 10 falls in your 9th house of higher consciousness. This ushers in a four-week cycle bolstering spirituality.

FINANCE
You will feel adventurous concerning your approach to financial decisions. Unpredictable Uranus impacts your 2nd house of money all year. You value money mostly for the freedom it promises. Technology can have a positive affect on your income. The winter, after Uranus goes direct on January 2, looks promising for financial gain.

Sites of Awe

Sekhmet Temple—Mojave Desert

THROUGH THE YEARS, *I have enjoyed visiting very special places in anticipation of writing the yearly Sites of Awe article. This year something different happened. While digging through my archives, I found this piece written in 2004, and decided to share it, along with an update from a phone conversation with a Priestess of the very captivating Sekhmet Temple.*

Well, I found myself in Las Vegas, Nevada, celebrating a 50th wedding anniversary with my family, when I learned about, and decided to visit, the Sekhmet temple in the Mojave Desert. After all, what better place to put a Sekhmet temple in the United States of America than in the desert?

While driving through Indian Springs, I see the left turn ahead that I need to take onto a dirt road. I hope this was worth the one-hour trip from Las Vegas. I am not a fan of the desert, the scorching sun or the heat. My rental car is kicking up a lot of sand, but I can still see a building in

the distance. Unfortunately, we have no cloud cover today, and it is hot!

As I approach, I see that the temple is quite small. The building stands only about 12-15 feet tall, with a large piece of metalwork on the top. The walls appear to be made of stucco and there are arched entrances located on more than one side. I did read somewhere that the temple was built in 1993 on a 20-acre parcel, located near the Nevada National Security Site (previously known as the Nevada Nuclear test site) and that on occasion, action-oriented visitors came to stay at the temple while protesting for peace. Now, I am anxious to see the inside, so I quickly park my car and get out into the sweltering heat! How did those Egyptians do it? Imagine building the pyramids in this heat.

Stepping inside, I find it a bit cooler. Wow, I'm a little surprised. Four entrances (one on each wall) align with the cross-quarters. Between each entrance is an altar aligned to a compass direction. I

think I was expecting everything to be focused toward one altar in the center. Best not to assume.

To the south (it's mid-day, and the Sun is up, so that one is easy), there is a beautiful statue of Sekhmet. She is decorated with red fabric and has flowers, candles and offerings at her feet. To the west is Our Lady of Guadalupe. To the north is Madre del Mundo. On the eastern wall, I'm fascinated to see a number of Goddess images from various cultures—a European Venus of Willendorf, Egyptian Isis, Tara and various others. In the center is a fire pit, and above it the ceiling is open, with a metallic ornamentation (appears to be copper) that was visible from outside.

The feeling in here is very alive— again, not what your average person might expect to find in the desert. But it is obvious to all of my senses that this place is visited often, and that energy has been raised here before. Taking a moment to settle into the atmosphere of the temple,

I hear prayers spoken, honoring the Mother expressed, offerings being left, songs being sung, incense burnt and candles lit. The temple is alive! It is not a big leap to imagine a fire lit in the center and shadows dancing on the walls. This is a place of serenity and of power. There is much more that can be said about the feeling and energy of the temple, but I believe it is flavored by each individual's personal relationship with the Goddess Sekhmet and the other deities represented here. I will be spending more time here before I have to leave. The temple provides a rare opportunity, and I just want to bask in the feeling of the powerful feminine a bit longer.

If you find yourself able to visit this very unique site, you will not be disappointed. I promise.

2016 Update: Now with a beautiful guesthouse which accommodates twelve, a priestess house, herbal garden, outdoor fire pit, space for workshops and much more, this temple has really grown. Each month, visitors can find workshops and rituals being hosted by the temple. The Full Moon, New Moon and Pagan holidays are recognized and open to the public. Some of their current projects involve mistletoe removal, sacred art trail and meditation path, outdoor art exhibit, drum circle mosaic art, artist trading cards, herb garden, beekeeping and more.

– ARMAND TABER

The Sekhmet Temple's website is filled with more information on Goddess Spirituality and happenings at the Temple. Truly a site rich in information. www.sekhmettemple.com

Reviews

Trance Journeys of the Hunter-Gatherers: Ecstatic Practices to Reconnect with the Great Mother and Heal the Earth
ISBN-13: 978-1591432371
Bear and Co.
$17.48

THOSE UNFAMILIAR with the work of Nicholas E. Brink should know he is a practicing psychologist whose focus for decades has been the transformative power of ecstatic trance. His present effort is no different in its outlook nor its candor. It is a voyage through different techniques of positive metamorphosis, practical and effective exercises of life and spirit-affirming change.

Partially a magical journal and partially a call to kindred souls to reconnect with the land and its ancestral spirits both human and animal, *Trance Journeys* relates dozens of transformative experiences recorded by mystical practitioners and case-study participants, showing how they were able to break through mental barriers and massive emotional blocks—some years in the making—through the power of chants, poses, breathing techniques and dynamic visualizations. Many of the techniques are Native American in scope and theme, though European egregores and deities such as Cernunnos will occasionally reveal themselves in the journals of the participants. Interspersed are snippets of wisdom and personal experiences related by the author himself, seamlessly tying them into each chapter with warmth and compassion.

Trance Journeys of the Hunter-Gatherers is a treasure of a book that inspires the reader to practice and achieve altered and ecstatic states of consciousness, transcending their fears with a guiding hand of foresight, clarity and understanding.

The English Magic Tarot
ISBN-978-1578636006
Weiser Books
$24.95

A NOD TO BRITISH occultists of the early modern period, the English Magic Tarot is a solid deck with a graphic novel feel. It is the collaboration of three artistic minds: Magician and comic book artist Rex Van Ryn, London painter Steve Dooley, and Andy Letcher, Druid and author of *Shroom: A Cultural History of the Magic Mushroom*.

It is interestingly a period tarot deck—cursorily dealing with historical happenings of the British Isles between Henry VIII's ascension to the throne (1509) and the death of Charles II (1685). Drawing from such brilliant and enigmatic occult personalities such as John Dee and Isaac Newton, the deck is very animated. Van Ryn's pen and ink work is highly dynamic, changing perspectives in a way that makes every card dance and bend, while Dooley's coloring is bold and simple—a series of solid base colors each with a bit of earthy grit to them, keeping the deck's feel rustic and warm.

The Major Arcana holds some great new twists on classic themes, while we are given a new series of wonderfully illustrative Minor Arcana cards, each with a thick bold border corresponding to their elemental attribution. The Majors remain borderless, but the entire deck from Fool to Page of Coins simply brims with life.

Viking Music

IF YOU ARE A FAN of the History Channel's series *Vikings* then you may be familiar with the music of the Norwegian group Wardruna. Basing their music on the Runes of the Elder Futhark, Wardruna holds fast to personal beliefs based in Ancient Nordic Folk Traditions and Spirituality. They have been producing a trilogy of albums each based on a set of Runes called *Runaljod* (The Sound of Runes)—*Gap Var Ginnunga* (2009), *Yggdrasil* (2013) and *Ragnarok* scheduled to be released in Autumn 2016. Their sound invokes dark ambient atmospherics and employs instruments that have been long lost to the modern musical experience. Many of them had to be built or crafted by hand. The project was created by Einar "Kvitrafn" Selvik who started his musical career in the Black Metal genre where he met his Wardruna collaborators Gaahl (a.k.a. Kristian Espedal) and vocalist Lindy Fay Hella. All still retain strong support within the Scandanavian and worldwide Metal community. A 2014 interview with Einar by an old friend Bret

Love of Green Global Travel is an excellent source of information about the band and their back story. It can be found at http://greenglobaltravel.com/2014/07/30/wardruna-einar-selvik-interview/ and the band's homepage can be found at Wardruna.com.

Fever Ray is another Scandanavian artist with a connection to the *Vikings* series. Fever Ray is an alias of Karin Dreijer Andersson who recorded originally as part of the Swedish electronic duo *The Knife*. "If I Had a Heart," one of four singles from her self-titled debut album is used in the *Vikings* title sequence. The brooding lyrics are perfectly framed by slow hypnotic beats and a relentless haunting drone. The vocals are delivered in a ghostly plaintive voice calling out from the kind of experience that can only be had in a classic shamanic underworld journey. The Youtube of the official music video release can be found at https://www.youtube.com/watch?v=EBAzlNJonO8.

The Witch: A New England Folktale

WRITTEN AND DIRECTED by Robert Eggers, *The Witch* debuted at the 2015 Sundance Film Festival and was also screened in the Special Presentations section of the 2015 Toronto International Film Festival. After its general release the film achieved globally positive reviews from critics. *The Witch* blurs the line between accuracy in depicting the harsh life and social constructs of the early New England Puritan experience, with a fanciful and at times grotesque passion play about the extreme beliefs and hysteria which led to the actual persecution and execution of Massachusetts Bay Colonists in the 17th century. It plays off the hyper-realistic attention to detail of the sets and costuming with a tale of fear and horror direct out of the fantasy world of the Puritan mind. There are scenes that depict the very worst imaginings of a demon-haunted culture which range from the disgusting to the fringes of ecstatic reverie.

The film features a most unusual supporting character, Black Phillip, who is both a large Black Goat with enormous horns and an enigmatic "Man in Black" Devil figure. The cast delivers their lines in perfect 17th century dialog and punctuates their somber existence with appropriately dour delivery. This can be criticized as slow and uneventful if you miss the point that the most exciting part of the characters' lives is the fear-based guilt smothering their basic humanity in a dense cloud of joyless anxiety. There are moments of explosive emotion which seethe and ripple just under the surface, creating a rolling wave of tension that carries you forward to the ultimate release of the final scene—itself a Goya-like representation which comes alive off the canvas. This isn't a film for dinner and a date. It IS a film for deep reflection and a warning those who abandon common sense and basic human values for the constraints of Dogma and the restrictive vision of an overly-managed social order allow no deviation from the mind control of a dominating culture. This is a film to experience not just read about. Prepare for conflicting feelings and reactions. And when the last scene unfolds just let it all go, trust me—when you get there you will know what I mean.

The Website of Sarah Anne Lawless
Sacred Artist and Herbalist
Sarahannelawless.com

THOSE WITCHES looking for a wonderful website to get lost in for hours should look no further than that of Sarah Anne Lawless. A Witch and Herbalist raised in the Pacific Northwest and now living in rural Ontario, Lawless has been providing brilliant articles and works of art for such prestigious occult publishers as Scarlet Imprint and Aeon Sophia Press, as well as contributing pieces for such well-known staples as *The Cauldron* and *Hex Magazine*. Her articles concerning witchcraft, herbalism, and the poison path are wonderfully informative without feeling verbose or prone to pedantry, and her gorgeous yet understated artwork, usually inks and prints, perpetually incorporate feathers, bones, sigils, skulls, entheogenic plants and other such mysteries of the wildwood.

Her blogs and foraging journals are treasure-troves of herbal advice and brilliant photography, helping anyone identify and work with the myriad growing plants that have become part and parcel of a traditional Witch's repertoire. In addition, she and a local friend have created Fern & Fungi Botanicals, a webstore offering wildcrafted teas, mushroom elixirs, flying ointments, herbal classes and more. If podcasts are more your speed, her Hedgefolk Tales are well worth a listen.

The interface itself is both stunning and well organized, with dozens of clickable images drawing the visitor into Sarah's personal journey through the Greenwood at every turn. A site to be placed at the top of the "favorites" list.

From a Witch's Mailbox

High or low?

What is the difference between ceremonial magic and cunning magic?—Submitted by Larry E. Flanders

Ceremonial magic (sometimes called high magic) is a rather broad term that encompasses many practices that have their origins in Western mystery schools developed during the Renaissance. During its golden era, the practices of Ceremonial magic, more often than not, involved elaborate exacting rituals meant to manipulate spirits. Cunning (sometimes called low magic), on the other hand, has survived through the work of the common folk. Their approach was rooted in common practices of folk that dealt with everyday problems and healing. The difference between Ceremonial and Cunning magic is like comparing lace work to quilting. They are both different and useful.

A practical approach

I am new to the Pagan path, how do I move from reading to practicing? Should I construct my own rituals?—Submitted by Sandra Blackburn

First let me say, welcome to a new and exciting journey! Taking your first steps into the realm of practicality will wholly depend on what you think ritual is.

Taking a walk in the forest can be as magically moving as much as a structured ritual can be. Allow your intuition to guide you as to how much of each will cause the change you are looking for. Constructing rituals can be fun. Begin with simple rituals such as lighting a candle and some incense and contemplating the wonder of the world you exist in. Read as many ritual scripts as you can, taking note of their structure, as well as words. If a particular format moves you, change it to fit your world view. Again, intuition should be your guide.

To magic or not

Is Witchcraft a type of religion or is it magic?—Submitted by Don Vella

There is no easy way to answer this question. There are many who say that witchcraft is simply magic which does not have a need for religious motif. There are some who see Witchcraft as a religion that uses magic. Both are correct, although in present day, most would define Witchcraft (upper case "w") as a nature based religion which uses magic and witchcraft (lower case "w") is folk magic devoid of religion.

To divine is to know

How often should someone use divination?—Submitted by Sheila Barns

This depends on what you are using divination for. Many will divine before doing spell work, each and every time.

The reasoning is that you want to know if it will be effective and if there are obstacles that need to be overcome for the work to be successful.

If you are doing divination for guidance for yourself, you can do it daily—for example a simple one card draw of the Tarot to guide you for the day. A full in depth divination should be performed less frequently, perhaps no more than once a month.

Is there a link?

Do I need a link to do spells that are for healing?—Submitted by Debbie Hall

Having a link when doing healing work can be very helpful. Using a link while doing healing is called sympathetic magic. The premise is that link is symbolically associated with the person over which influence is sought. Because a piece of hair or nail clipping is in sympathy with the person from whom it is obtained, any magic directed at it will affect them. You can of course do the magic without the link, but why not increase effectiveness if you can?

I see ghosts

I see spirits and energy patterns all of the time, is this common?—Submitted by Dana Jones

This is not as uncommon as some may believe. There are individuals that are more open to energy and spirits than others. Within the more preceptive group there are those that can see in more detail than others. There are also

those who sense energy and spirits rather than seeing. The danger of being sensitive is not being able to turn it off. If you find this gift to be a distraction at times, you might want to learn how to ground and center. Otherwise, enjoy it and make sure you keep a good journal you can review over time.

Let us hear from you, too

We love to hear from our readers. Letters should be sent with the writer's name (or just first name or initials), address, daytime phone number and e-mail address, if available. Published material may be edited for clarity or length. All letters and e-mails will become the property of The Witches' Almanac Ltd. *and will not be returned. We regret that due to the volume of correspondence we cannot reply to all communications.*

The Witches' Almanac, Ltd.
P.O. Box 1292
Newport, RI 02840-9998
info@TheWitchesAlmanac.com
www.TheWitchesAlmanac.com

Aradia
Gospel of the Witches
Charles Godfrey Leland

ARADIA IS THE FIRST work in English in which witchcraft is portrayed as an underground old religion, surviving in secret from ancient pagan times.

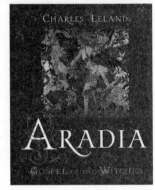

- Used as a core text by many modern neo-pagans.
- Foundation material containing traditional witchcraft practices
- This special edition features appreciations by such authors and luminaries as Paul Huson, Raven Grimassi, Judika Illes, Michael Howard, Christopher Penczak, Myth Woodling, Christina Oakley Harrington, Patricia Della-Piana, Jimahl di Fiosa and Donald Weiser. A beautiful and compelling work, this edition has brought the format up to date, while keeping the text unchanged. 172 pages $16.95

❧ *Expanded classics!* ☙

The ABC of Magic Charms
Elizabeth Pepper

SINCE THE DAWN of mankind, an obscure instinct in the human spirit has sought protection from mysterious forces beyond mortal control. Human beings sought benefaction in the three realms that share Earth with us — animal, mineral, vegetable. All three, humanity discovered, contain mysterious properties discovered over millennia through occult divination. An enlarged edition of *Magic Charms from A to Z*, compiled by the staff of *The Witches' Almanac*. $12.95

The Little Book of Magical Creatures
Elizabeth Pepper and Barbara Stacy

A loving tribute to the animal kingdom

AN UPDATE of the classic *Magical Creatures*, featuring Animals Tame, Animals Wild, Animals Fabulous – plus an added section of enchanting animal myths from other times, other places. *A must for all animal lovers.* $12.95

♣ a lady shape-shifts into a white doe ♣ two bears soar skyward
♣ Brian Boru rides a wild horse ♣ a wolf growls dire prophecy

The Witchcraft of Dame Darrel of York

Charles Godfrey Leland

Introduction by Robert Mathiesen

The Witches' Almanac presents:

- *A previously unpublished work by folklorist Charles Godfrey Leland.*
- *Published in full color facsimile with a text transcript.*
- *Forward by Prof. Robert Mathiesen.*

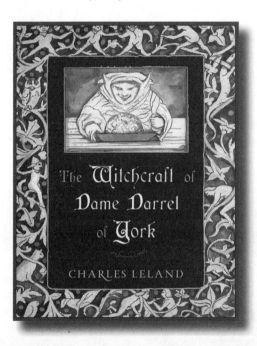

This beautifully reproduced facsimile of the illuminated manuscript will shed light on an ancient tradition as well as provide the basis for a modern practice. It will be treasured by those practicing Pagans, scholars, and all those fascinated by the legend and lore of England.

Standard hardcover edition ($65.00).
Deluxe numbered edition with slipcase ($85.00).
Exclusive full leather bound, numbered and slip cased edition ($145.00).

For further information visit http://TheWitchesAlmanac.com/damedarrel.html

Available from Olympian Press...

The Rede of the Wiccae

Adriana Porter, Gwen Thompson
and the birth of a tradition of witchcraft

by Robert Mathiesen and Theitic

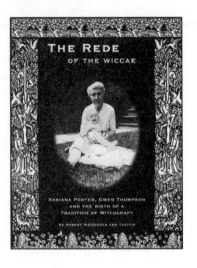

This is a tale told by Gwen Thompson about her grandmother, Adriana Porter, and how she came to be the last carrier of her ancestral tradition of Witchcraft.

The information was researched by Robert Mathiesen, a medieval philologist and professor at Brown University, and Theitic, an elder in the tradition that Gwen Thompson founded.

$49.95 Hardcover plus $4 S & H

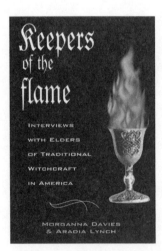

Keepers of the Flame

Interviews with elders of traditional witchcraft in America

by Morganna Davies and Aradia Lynch

Many traditional witches have deliberately avoided all the fanfare and media hype that some who call themselves "witches" seem to covet. Some have preferred to remain anonymous, quietly practicing their Craft and passing the tradition on to their students. These elders are growing older and the torches are being passed to a new generation.

This book is not about the elders, it is a record of their opinions, views, comments and ideas of what the Craft was, what it is today, and what they think it will be in the future.
$20.95 plus $3 S & H — 216 pages

The products and services offered above are paid advertisements.

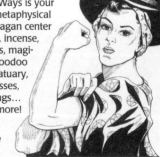

The products and services offered above are paid advertisements.

The BIG Little Book of L♥ve Magic

978-1-57863-592-4, $16.95

Let's face it, we are obsessed, inspired, delighted, and in love with love. And here is the go-to book for every spell you will ever need for finding and keeping romance, passion, sex, marriage, fertility, and love in your life. Rooted in serious scholarship while still exploring the weird, wild, and wonderful side of love magic, this book provides expert advice and genuine spells that work to bring you your heart's desire.

❧Marketplace❧

www.angelsofchiron.com Angels * Candles * Magic & More. We Believe That Every Sign Can Get Along! We do Google & Facebook. For Astrology & Angel Card Readings email angelsofchiron74@gmail.com and ask for Becky.

www.azuregreen.net Jewelry, Amulets, Incense, Oils, Herbs, Candles, Statuary, Gemstones, Ritual Items. Over 8,000 items.

Voodoo Queen specializing in removal and reversal of evil spells. Be careful of what you wish for before you call me: **678-677-1144**

The products and services offered above are paid advertisements.

TO: The Witches' Almanac
P.O. Box 1292, Newport, RI 02840-9998
www.TheWitchesAlmanac.com

Name_____

Address_____

City_____ State_____ Zip_____

E-mail_____

WITCHCRAFT being by nature one of the secretive arts, it may not be as easy to find us next year. If you'd like to make sure we know where you are, why don't you send us your name and address? You will certainly hear from us.

The Witches' Almanac Coloring Book

Gwion Vran and
Ydal Nevrom

The Witches' Almanac presents:

• *96 Black and white images for coloring.*

• *A brief introduction to the contents of each section.*

• *Historic woodcuts and 22 Major Arcana and the four Aces of the Tarot.*

The Witches' Almanac has long featured black and white images of beautiful woodcuts, fantastical creatures, tarot cards, astrological features and constellations, as well as line drawing selected from the folklore of our global community. The Witches' Almanac Coloring Book brings together a lager format of these images presented in past Almanacs (in addition to images that have not been presented) allowing the inner artist to emerge in a mediation of color.

112 pages — $12.00

For further information visit http://TheWitchesAlmanac.com/

MAGIC

An Occult Primer

David Conway

The Witches' Almanac presents:

- *A clear articulate presentation of magic in a workable format*
- *Updated text, graphics and appendicest*
- *Forward by Colin Wilson.*

David Conway's *Magic: An Occult Primer* is a seminal work that brought magical training to the every-magician in the early 70s. David is an articulate writer presenting the mysteries in a very workable manner for the serious student. Along with the updated texts on philosophy and practical magic is a plethora of graphics that have all been redrawn, promising to be another collector's edition published by The Witches' Almanac.

384 pages — $24.95

For further information visit http://TheWitchesAlmanac.com//anoccultprimer.html

ANCIENT ROMAN HOLIDAYS

The glory that was Rome awaits you in Barbara Stacy's classic presentation of a festive year in pagan times. Here are the gods and goddesses as the Romans conceived them, accompanied by the annual rites performed in their worship. Scholarly, light-hearted – a rare combination.

CELTIC TREE MAGIC

Robert Graves in *The White Goddess* writes of the significance of trees in the old Celtic lore. *Celtic Tree Magic* is an investigation of the sacred trees in the remarkable Beth-Luis-Nion alphabet; their role in folklore, poetry, and mysticism.

MOON LORE

As both the largest and the brightest object in the night sky, and the only one to appear in phases, the Moon has been a rich source of myth for as long as there have been mythmakers.

MAGIC SPELLS
AND INCANTATIONS

Words have magic power. Their sound, spoken or sung, has ever been a part of mystic ritual. From ancient Egypt to the present, those who practice the art of enchantment have drawn inspiration from a treasury of thoughts and themes passed down through the ages.

LOVE FEASTS

Creating meals to share with the one you love can be a sacred ceremony in itself. With the witch in mind, culinary adept Christine Fox offers magical menus and recipes for every month in the year.

RANDOM RECOLLECTIONS
II, III, IV

Pages culled from the original (no longer available) issues of *The Witches' Almanac,* published annually throughout the 1970's, are now available in a series of tasteful booklets. A treasure for those who missed us the first time around; keepsakes for those who remember.

A Treasury from past editions...

Witches All

Perfect for study or casual reading, Witches All *is a collection from* The Witches' Almanac *publications of the past. Arranged by topics, the book, like the popular almanacs, is thought provoking and often spurs me on to a tangent leading to even greater discovery. The information and art in the book – astrological attributes, spells, recipes, history, facts & figures is a great reminder of the history of the Craft, not just in recent years, but in the early days of the Witchcraft Revival in this century: the witch in an historical and cultural perspective.* Ty Bevington, Circle of the Wicker Man, Columbus, Ohio

Absolutely beautiful! I recently ordered Witches All *and I have to say I wasn't disappointed. The artwork and articles are first rate and for a longtime* Witches' Almanac *fan, it is a wonderful addition to my collection.* Witches' Almanac *devotees and newbies alike will love this latest effort. Very worth getting.*

Tarot3, Willits, California

GREEK GODS IN LOVE

Barbara Stacy casts a marvelously original eye on the beloved stories of Greek deities, replete with amorous oddities and escapades. We relish these tales in all their splendor and antic humor, and offer an inspired storyteller's fresh version of the old, old mythical magic.

MAGIC CHARMS FROM A TO Z

A treasury of amulets, talismans, fetishes and other lucky objects compiled by the staff of *The Witches' Almanac*. An invaluable guide for all who respond to the call of mystery and enchantment.

LOVE CHARMS

Love has many forms, many aspects. Ceremonies performed in witchcraft celebrate the joy and the blessings of love. Here is a collection of love charms to use now and ever after.

MAGICAL CREATURES

Mystic tradition grants pride of place to many members of the animal kingdom. Some share our life. Others live wild and free. Still others never lived at all, springing instead from the remarkable power of human imagination.

News from The Witches' Almanac

Glad tidings from the staff

Well, we have some exciting news for you this year. First, we would like to thank Karen Marks for her years of dedication as *The Witches' Almanac's* Art Director. Her presence will surely be missed. We would also like to wish her well in her future endeavors. Thank you Karen!

Second, we would like to welcome Gwion Vran as the new Art Director! Gwion comes to *The Witches' Almanac* with an extensive background in the design field. We look forward to seeing his experience unfold in our upcoming publications. In fact, you can already see some of his work by checking out *The Witches' Almanac Coloring Book*—thank you Gwion!

This past year, *The Witches' Almanac* published two additional titles—*Magic: An Occult Primer* by David Conway (a new and expanded version of the original 1972 classic edition) and *The Witches' Almanac Coloring Book* (a collection of woodcuts and fantastic, magical images). Watch for other new titles in the fall and winter of 2016–2017.

With the growth of *The Witches' Almanac* and the addition of new titles, we have also found it spot-on to add another staff member. Please welcome Anthony Teth as a writer and lead editor. With a strong background in everything magical, he is a superlative addition to our growing and already knowledgeable staff.

You have asked for it, and you will get it...*The Witches' Almanac* will be rolling out a new shopping cart before the end of 2016! It promises to have many bells and whistles, allowing us to promote special reductions, bundle discounts and more (also allowing us to occasionally offer free shipping on select titles). The new flexibility of our shopping cart will be active at the same time as our new web site is launched! *The Witches' Almanac's* site has grown over the years, with new products, titles and information. It is now time to reorganize our site, to offer you a simpler way to find what you are looking for, and to add some exciting new features!

As always, we are happy to be working with you, our readership. In an effort to improve your experience with *The Witches' Almanac*, we will continue to grow and evolve as the magical community does.

Order Form

Each timeless edition of *The Witches' Almanac* is unique.
Limited numbers of previous years' editions are available.

Item	Price	Qty.	Total
2017-2018 The Witches' Almanac – Water	$12.95		
2016-2017 The Witches' Almanac – Air	$12.95		
2015-2016 The Witches' Almanac – Fire	$12.95		
2014-2015 The Witches' Almanac – Earth	$12.95		
2013-2014 The Witches' Almanac – Moon	$11.95		
2012-2013 The Witches' Almanac – Sun	$11.95		
2011-2012 The Witches' Almanac – Stones, Powers of Earth	$11.95		
2010-2011 The Witches' Almanac – Animals Great & Small	$11.95		
2009-2010 The Witches' Almanac – Plants & Healing Herbs	$11.95		
2008-2009 The Witches' Almanac – Divination & Prophecy	$10.95		
2007-2008 The Witches' Almanac – Water	$9.95		
2006-2007 The Witches' Almanac – Air	$8.95		
2005-2006 The Witches' Almanac – Fire	$8.95		
2004-2005 The Witches' Almanac – Earth	$8.95		
2003-2004 The Witches' Almanac – Air	$8.95		
1999, 2000, 2001, 2002 issues of The Witches' Almanac	$7.95		
1995, 1996, 1997, 1998 issues of The Witches' Almanac	$6.95		
1993, 1994 issues of The Witches' Almanac	$5.95		
Magic: An Occult Primer	$24.95		
The Witches' Almanac Coloring Book	$12.00		
The Witchcraft of Dame Darrel of York, clothbound	$65.00		
Aradia or The Gospel of the Witches	$16.95		
The Horned Shepherd	$16.95		
The ABC of Magic Charms	$12.95		
The Little Book of Magical Creatures	$12.95		
Greek Gods in Love	$15.95		
Witches All	$13.95		
Ancient Roman Holidays	$6.95		
Celtic Tree Magic	$7.95		
Love Charms	$6.95		
Love Feasts	$6.95		
Magic Charms from A to Z	$12.95		
Magical Creatures	$12.95		
Magic Spells and Incantations	$7.95		
Moon Lore	$7.95		
Random Recollections II, III or IV (circle your choices)	$3.95		
SALE 20 Almanac back issues with free book bag and free shipping	$100.00		
The Rede of the Wiccae – Hardcover only	$49.95		
Keepers of the Flame	$20.95		
Subtotal			
Tax *(7% sales tax for RI customers)*			
Shipping & Handling *(See shipping rates section)*			
TOTAL			

BRACELETS

Item	Price	Qty.	Total
Agate, Green	$5.95		
Agate, Moss	$5.95		
Agate, Natural	$5.95		
Agate, Red	$5.95		
Aventurine	$5.95		
Fluorite	$5.95		
Jade, African	$5.95		
Jade, White	$5.95		
Jasper, Picture	$5.95		
Jasper, Red	$5.95		
Malachite	$5.95		
Onyx, Black	$5.95		
Quartz Crystal	$5.95		
Rhodonite	$5.95		
Sodalite	$5.95		
Unakite	$5.95		
Subtotal			
Tax (7% for RI customers)			
Shipping & Handling *(See shipping rates section)*			
TOTAL			

MISCELLANY

Item	Price	Qty.	Total
Pouch	$3.95		
Matches: *10 small individual boxes*	$5.00		
Matches: *1 large box of 50 individual boxes*	$20.00		
Natural/Black Book Bag	$17.95		
Red/Black Book Bag	$17.95		
Hooded Sweatshirt, Blk	$30.00		
Hooded Sweatshirt, Red	$30.00		
L-Sleeve T, Black	$20.00		
L-Sleeve T, Red	$20.00		
S-Sleeve T, Black/W	$15.00		
S-Sleeve T, Black/R	$15.00		
S-Sleeve T, Dk H/R	$15.00		
S-Sleeve T, Dk H/W	$15.00		
S-Sleeve T, Red/B	$15.00		
S-Sleeve T, Ash/R	$15.00		
S-Sleeve T, Purple/W	$15.00		
Postcards – set of 12	$3.00		
Bookmarks – set of 12	$1.00		
Magnets – set of 3	$1.50		
Promo Pack	$7.00		
Subtotal			
Tax (7% sales tax for RI customers)			
Shipping & Handling *(See shipping rates section)*			
TOTAL			

SHIPPING & HANDLING CHARGES

BOOKS: One book, add $5.95. Each additional book add $1.50.

POUCH: One pouch, $3.95. Each additional pouch add $1.50.

MATCHES: Ten individual boxes, add $3.95.
One large box of fifty, add $6.00. Each additional large box add $7.95.

BOOKBAGS: $5.95 per bookbag.

BRACELETS: $3.95 per bracelet.

Send a check or money order payable in U. S. funds or credit card details to:

The Witches' Almanac, Ltd., PO Box 1292, Newport, RI 02840-9998

(401) 847-3388 (phone) • (888) 897-3388 (fax)
Email: info@TheWitch[...]lmanac.com